Dedication

To My Son

Keanu, I hope that one day you'll read this book and see the life your mom and I built with intention—not just to live a "rich life" by the world's standards, but to create a legacy of love, strength, generosity, and purpose.

May the values we've lived by inspire you to build even bigger things. Use what we've built as your foundation, but trust your heart and please never stop chasing whatever dreams and goals fill your head.

I don't know where you are or how old you are when you're reading this, but know this: I love you more than words could ever express. Watching you grow has been the greatest joy of my life, second only to marrying your mom. I couldn't be more proud or grateful to call an amazing kid like you my son.

Whatever path you choose, we'll always be behind you—cheering you on, lifting you up, and believing in you every step of the way. You may grow to be as tall and strong as a tree, but you'll always be my little monkey.

Love,

Dad

To My Amazing Wife

Thank you for believing in me long before there was proof—before clients, before systems, before any of this made sense on paper. You said yes to the adventure: passports and carry-ons, new cities and unfamiliar beds, early flights with a sleepy kid, and late nights while I chased one more idea.

You've been the steady heartbeat of our family while I've tried to build something worthy of your faith in me.

This book exists because of all the ups and downs we've navigated together trying to build the life of our dreams. You gave me courage when doubt got loud, perspective when my plans got too big, and grace when they took longer than I promised. You turned my dreams into our life, and our life into something we can pass on.

Thank you for your patience, your partnership, your fierce love, and the way you make every place we land feel like home. You are my favorite adventure and the one place my heart feels safest. Everything I do, I do for you.

Love,
Your King

To Every Reader

My hope for you is that you find something—or someone—that gives you the strength to keep going when life tests you. There will be seasons when things feel uncertain, when progress feels slow, and when quitting seems easier than continuing. Don't. Keep showing up. Keep believing in what you're building, even when no one else can see it yet. Because that's what this entire journey is really about—staying true to your vision long enough for it to become a reality.

From ~~REGULAR~~ to RICH

How One Decision Can Transform Your Financial Life Forever

SHAWN M KING

ISBN: 979-8-90057-141-6 - Ebook

ISBN: 979-8-90057-142-3 - Paperback

ISBN: 979-8-90057-143-0 - Hardcover

GET YOUR FREE GIFTS!

To get the most out of this book, I recommend downloading and using **Our Free 7 Steps to Becoming the Banker**, **our Monthly Budget Template**, and **our Legacy Trust Outline**. Readers who use these resources alongside the book typically implement the steps more quickly and gain clarity faster as they begin their journey *From Regular to Rich..*

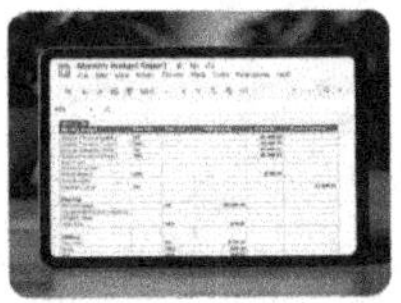

You can get a copy of all three by visiting:
www.LegacyLifeandRetirement.com

Connect with me on social media by scanning the QR code below:

CONTENTS

FOREWORD

By Jeremiah Dew

There are two kinds of people who talk about money.

The first kind talks about—numbers, noise, and narratives borrowed from someone else's success. The second kind talks through it—using money as a lens to examine life, values, tradeoffs, and truth.

Shawn King is firmly in the second camp.

I've had the privilege of working alongside Shawn for the past few years inside The Cash Compound, and in that time I've come to appreciate something rare: he doesn't just study financial concepts—he submits his life to them. He tests ideas in real time. He stress-tests principles against raising kids, real-world demands, and shifting priorities. And when something doesn't hold up in real life, he doesn't defend it—he discards it.

That posture alone makes this book worth your time.

Shawn is an authorized practitioner with the Nelson Nash Institute, deeply committed to the Infinite Banking Concept, he's savvy on social media, fluent in finance, and unmistakably a deep thinker. But credentials aren't what qualify him to write From Regular to Rich. Character is. Consistency is. Curiosity is. The willingness to ask uncomfortable questions and sit with inconvenient answers.

This book didn't come from a mountaintop revelation. It came from the margin. From moments between responsibility and rest. From the quiet realization that doing "what you're supposed to do" doesn't always produce the life you hoped it would. Shawn didn't wake up one day rich and decide to explain it. He woke up regular—and decided to rethink everything.

What you'll feel as you read this isn't hype. It's honesty.

And honesty is refreshing in a financial world that often sells certainty it can't deliver.

One of the things I respect most about Shawn is that he doesn't treat money as a finish line. He treats it as a tool—powerful, yes, but dangerous when misunderstood. He understands that money amplifies who you already are. If you're reactive, it makes you reckless. If you're intentional, it makes you influential. If you're unclear, it makes you anxious. And if you're aligned, it becomes an ally.

That understanding permeates every page.

This is Shawn's first published work, and you can tell—not because it lacks polish, but because it overflows with purpose. The words are not borrowed. They're built. They come from lived experience, late-night conversations, spreadsheets that forced humility, and decisions that required faith before they produced fruit.

You won't find jargon without context here. You won't find theory without application. And you won't find a single page that treats the reader like a prospect instead of a person.

That matters.

Because the truth is, most people don't need more information—they need better integration. They don't need louder voices; they need clearer ones. They don't need to be impressed; they need to be empowered.

Shawn understands this, which is why the tone of this book feels less like a lecture and more like a conversation—one that respects where you are while refusing to leave you there.

As a coach, Shawn brings clarity. As a practitioner, he brings credibility. As a husband and father, he brings context. And as a teacher, he brings restraint—never rushing the process, never overstating the promise, never underestimating the reader.

That balance is rare.

And it's especially rare in a culture addicted to acceleration.

What I hope you notice as you read is not just what Shawn teaches, but how he thinks. He doesn't chase financial freedom as an escape from responsibility; he pursues it as a way to engage more fully with it. He doesn't talk about legacy as something reserved for the wealthy; he treats it as a responsibility for the willing. He doesn't confuse movement with progress or income with independence.

In short, he's done the slow work of alignment—and that work shows.

Writing a foreword like this is a first for me as well, and I don't take it lightly. You only lend your voice to work you believe in, written by people you trust, for readers you care about. This book checks all three boxes.

If you're looking for shortcuts, this isn't your book.

If you're looking for clarity, it might be.

If you're tired of being busy but not building, earning but not owning, succeeding but not satisfied—this book may meet you right on time.

From Regular to Rich doesn't promise transformation without effort. It offers something better: a framework for thinking differently, acting deliberately, and building patiently. It respects the reader enough to tell the truth—that real wealth is less about speed and more about stewardship.

So read slowly. Reflect honestly. And don't rush past the moments that make you uncomfortable—they're usually the ones doing the most work.

Shawn didn't write this book to impress you.

He wrote it to invite you—to rethink, to realign, and to redesign a life that feels as good on the inside as it looks on paper.

That's not just rare.

That's rich.

I hope you get everything you need from this book and you let it be a turning point not only in your financial life but your life as a whole.

My Wake-Up Call

Most people don't choose to be stuck; they just don't have a better plan. This book is meant to be that better plan.

If you were to meet me in person, you might not believe we have much in common, but I promise, we're more alike than you realize.

I didn't grow up poor, but I sure as hell didn't grow up rich either. My family landed somewhere in the middle. While money wasn't a taboo subject in my house, it wasn't something we openly talked about. I got the typical "Money doesn't grow on trees" line, and that was the extent of my financial education. Don't get me wrong, I have incredible parents. It's just hard to teach your children something you weren't taught yourself.

Growing up in the nineties, success in my eyes was defined by what I saw on TV. To be honest, I was heavily influenced by the *MTV Cribs* lifestyle. The big houses, flashy cars, designer clothes, and those huge stacks of cash that never seemed to run out. I thought if I could just make it to the NBA or become a wildly successful businessman, that lifestyle would be mine. While you may or may not be able to relate to that, we've all had dreams of who we *thought* we would become.

I did end up having the opportunity to play Division 1 basketball on a full-ride scholarship, but the NBA definitely wasn't in the cards for me. To be blunt, I wasn't nearly good enough. So after college, I did what a lot of people do: I got a "decent" job. Then another one. Then another, and somewhere along the line, I started asking myself: Why do I still feel broke? Why am I working so hard, but never getting ahead?

There were months I'd check my bank account and there it was, a big, fat $0 staring back at me. It wasn't for lack of effort. I've always had the drive and hunger to succeed, but what I didn't have was the right plan. Even though I had a degree, I didn't feel like I had the right education to set me up for real financial success. I was living paycheck to paycheck, juggling credit card debt, and wondering how in the world people actually built real wealth. Like most people, I believed I was meant to achieve more; I just hadn't found the path yet.

To make matters worse, the world around me kept pushing the same outdated message. Please stop me if you've heard this one before:

- ✔ Go to school.
- ✔ Get a good job.
- ✔ Work hard.
- ✔ Put your money in a 401(k).
- ✔ Retire at sixty-five.
- ✔ Cross your fingers and hope it doesn't all blow up in your face.

But the reality is that 60 percent of Americans live paycheck to paycheck (LendingClub 2024),[1] and that includes people earning six figures. If you want an idea of how well this system works, consider this: According to a 2023 Federal Reserve study, only 37 percent of people feel they're on track to reach their retirement goals.[2]

I don't know about you, but I've never been a fan of blindly following rules, especially once I started realizing who made them. After college, while working multiple jobs that felt like they were getting me nowhere, I began examining how our financial system really worked, simply because I was tired of being broke. The deeper I looked, the more obvious it became that the game was rigged, and not in our favor.

Have you ever decided you wanted to buy a new car, then all of a sudden you see that same style car everywhere you go? Something similar happened to me with money. I started to realize that banks, the government, and all these talking-head financial "experts" kept telling me to trust the system—the same system failing countless others right before my eyes.

That's when things started to shift.

At the time, I was working in sales. One of the few benefits of that job was the company's emphasis on personal development. I picked up my first real book on money (*Rich Dad Poor Dad* by Robert Kiyosaki), and for the first time ever, I actually wanted to read. That book led to more books, then podcasts, mentors, and masterminds. Piece by piece, the puzzle started coming together.

---

1   LendingClub Corporation. *Paycheck-to-Paycheck Report: The State of Consumers and the Economy.* February 2024. https://www.lendingclub.com/company/press/press-releases

2   Board of Governors of the Federal Reserve System. *Economic Well-Being of U.S Households in 2023 – May 2024.* Washington, D.C.: Federal Reserve, 2024. https://www.federalreserve.gov/publications/2024-economic-well-being-of-us-households-in-2023.htm

I began to realize that the wealthy don't follow the same rules regular people were taught. They own things. They control cash flow. They pass down values, not just valuables. And most importantly, they think long term.

I thought to myself, *What the hell? Why wasn't I taught this stuff in college?* From that point on, I committed to learning how the wealthy think and act so I could begin building a life that actually made sense to me. Not one based on "retirement" at sixty-five, but rather, freedom at every stage of life. There was no way I was going to work forty years of my life just to enjoy fifteen. Instead, I wanted to create a life where I could design each year around my family, my values, and my purpose—and I want to help you do the same.

A Truth You Need to Hear

You don't have to be a genius to build wealth. You just need a better plan. That's exactly what this book is going to provide you with.

If you've ever felt like you're working hard but getting nowhere...

If you've ever looked at your income and wondered why your savings never actually increases...

If you've ever thought to yourself, *There has to be a better way...*

You're in the right place.

Let me be clear about something though: Building wealth is quiet, patient work. This is not a book on how to get rich quick. If you're reading this because you're looking for overnight results, I'll save you the disappointment. You'd be better off trying to become an overnight sensation by doing something stupid on TikTok.

I'm not saying you're going to need thirty years, but if you're not willing to commit the next five to ten years, to be blunt with you, you're wasting your time. Think about it this way: Time is going to pass no matter what you do. You could either be miles ahead of where you're currently at, or you could be in a very similar situation just older, most likely fatter, and probably in a bit more pain, all while you're still stressing about your money. Luckily, it's your choice.

My Goal for You

My goal is simple: to show you how to build something that lasts.

→ A system that works even when you're sleeping.

→ A mindset that gives you clarity.

→ A strategy that gives your family options, not just obligations.

I call it going *From Regular to Rich*.

If it was possible for me, just a regular guy with a wife, a new baby boy, a dream, and some relentless belief and dedication, it's absolutely possible for you too, but you've got to be willing to work for it. Your dreams are your dreams for a reason. You're the only one who can make them a reality.

The Legacy Lifestyle Process

Most books hand you a bunch of ideas and send you on your way. This one gives you an actual system. The Legacy Lifestyle Process is the simple, repeatable framework I use with my own family and with the people I work with to move from "working harder" to designing a life of freedom.

It's built for regular people with real bills and real goals—no magic, no hype, no bullshit. Just four steps that stack one on top of the other. That's the path to go *From Regular to Rich*.

Step One - Recover and Redirect Your Cash

Find and fix the leaks in your financial bucket. Plug holes, realign spending, and redeploy your savings with a simple Four-Bucket Budget so your money starts moving with actual purpose instead of disappearing into thin air.

Step Two - Family Banking

Build your "Warehouse of Wealth" using one of the most flexible financial assets available—one that allows you to store your cash, keep it compounding, and borrow against it to fund life and opportunities without interrupting that growth.

Step Three - The Income Multiplier

Deploy your dollars into safe, strategic cash-flow opportunities like private lending, real estate partnerships, and mortgage note lending. Learn how to leverage Other People's Money (OPM) to multiply your returns while still maintaining control. This is where things get really fun.

Step Four - Legacy Protection

Protect what you've built using asset protection strategies like long-term care, smart business entities, and properly structured trusts so your values and wealth outlive you on purpose, not by accident.

The Knowledge You'll Gain

By the time you finish this book, I want you to *know* how money really works, *have* a personal system that puts you in control, and *be able to* build wealth with confidence—without relying on banks, employers, or the stock market to save you. My goal is to help you develop the clarity and discipline that separate those who simply survive from those who truly thrive. You'll learn how to manage cash flow like a banker, grow wealth like an investor, and protect your family's future like a legacy builder.

But more than that, I want you to understand what I eventually discovered—that regular people can build extraordinary lives when they stop following broken rules and start thinking differently. This isn't about chasing money; it's about mastering it. It's about creating freedom, not just income, and designing a life that reflects your values, not someone else's.

You'll come away from this book with the tools, systems, and mindset to make that possible. So if you're ready to trade confusion for clarity and take full control of your financial story, let's begin. Chapter 1 is where we start redefining what success really means.

Redefining Success

You're not failing. You just might be chasing someone else's dream.

Now that you understand my story and why I wrote this book, let's address the most important question you'll face on this journey: What does being "rich" look like to you?

Not what Instagram says.

Not what your neighbor says.

Not what eighteen-year-old you used to think it meant.

What does it actually look like right now?

Take a second and list out seven things that make you happy in the space below. No, seriously, do it.

1. ____

2. ____

3. _______________________________

4. _______________________________

5. _______________________________

6. _______________________________

7. _______________________________

How many of those things cost money? How many are free?

If you're like most people, your definition of success probably used to include things like a big house, expensive cars, luxury vacations, and a bank account with a whole lot of zeros. You've been conditioned your whole life to believe that success equals more: more money, more possessions, more status. Everyone is constantly trying to outdo those around them.

As Will Rogers said, "Too many people spend money they haven't earned, to buy things they don't want, to impress people they don't like."

You might think that having more money would mean fewer problems, right?

Wrong. I believe one of the greatest rappers alive, Notorious B.I.G., once said, "Mo Money Mo Problems."

You see, I've worked with clients who make $500,000 a year and are still stressed about time, overwhelmed by taxes, burdened by debt from poor decisions, and living according to someone else's schedule. Making more money doesn't always equal more happiness. What seems to matter most is how much control and clarity you have in your life.

My Definition of Rich

I wrote this book to help people understand that being rich isn't just about having money. Yes, money matters—there's no need to pretend it doesn't. But what if, instead of chasing a number, you pursued what gives your life that feeling of true richness? If you master these first four aspects of a rich life, I believe the financial piece will naturally follow.

To be rich is to be overflowing in the things that matter most, which include being:

- **Rich in relationships**. Your marriage, your bond with your children, the friends you share laughs with, and the family and community you pour into. These are the people who will be there for you when you need them most.

- **Rich in mindset**. Knowing how to quiet your doubts and move forward based on what you believe to be right and true.

- **Rich in experiences**. Whether these are experiences you create alone or with loved ones, having the ability to show up and be not only present but engaged will create much more meaning and enjoyment throughout your life.

- **Rich in contribution**. Supporting causes you believe in with the hope that you're making a lasting impact on those less fortunate than yourself.

- **Rich in finance**. Time freedom, cash flow, and wealth that lasts are still primary goals. But building that wealth through something you're passionate about, something that gives your life purpose, that's the *ultimate* goal.

"When you align your resources with your values, money becomes a tool, not a tyrant." – Jesse Mecham, *You Need a Budget*

The Myth of More

You must understand when enough is enough, because if you don't, you may become wealthy, but you'll never be rich.

Some of the most financially successful people I know—people who make more money than one family could ever need—have expressed a lack of fulfillment in their lives when their focus was centered around chasing dollars and growing their businesses. They realized that until they created an "exit strategy" for themselves and became easy to replace, they would never have the time to do what actually made them feel rich, which was spending time doing what they loved with the people they loved.

Think about that for a minute. These are people who "made it" by every traditional measure, and they still felt like something was missing.

Rewiring Your Metrics

How are you measuring success today? If it's by income alone, you're going to miss the mark.

If it's by how much time you spend with your children, how much peace you feel when you go to bed at night, and how excited you are to wake up and approach your work, that's something worth striving for.

Reflection Exercise

Finish these statements:

→ I feel most fulfilled when I'm…

____

→ My ideal week would include more

____

and less _______________________________________

→ If I could only pass down three lessons to my children
or future children, they would be: _______________

____

____

____

At this point, you should be starting to develop a better understanding of what a rich life looks like for you. Here's the beautiful thing: Once you get clear on what you're actually building toward, the "how" becomes a lot easier to figure out.

STEP ONE

RECOVER AND REDIRECT YOUR CASH

CHAPTER 2

Getting Clear on Your Budget

You can't build a rich life with a poor mindset, and you can't control your future if you don't control your cash flow.

Before you can build wealth, before you can leverage other people's money, before you can "become the bank," you have to know where your money is going.

That sounds obvious, right? Unfortunately, most people are flying blind. They work hard, earn a decent income, and still end up asking the same question at the end of every month: "Where did it all go?"

That question haunted my wife Amanda and me early on in our journey. We weren't broke, but we weren't moving forward either. We made decent money, yet we always felt like we were behind. The real issue was we had no system.

We didn't track our spending.

We didn't define our goals.

We didn't have a plan.

Everything shifted when we focused on becoming more intentional with our money. That meant building a monthly budget, tracking it, reviewing it, and treating it as a non-negotiable habit we committed to together.

That one practice, sitting down together at the end of every month to review our income and expenses, completely changed our financial life.

Let's get this out of the way right now: Budgeting is not about restriction. It's not about saying no to every coffee or canceling every membership you enjoy. Budgeting is about alignment.

When done correctly, your budget isn't a cage; it's a compass. It helps you stop spending money on things that don't matter so you can spend more freely on things that do. It's not about being cheap; it's about being intentional with your decisions.

That's the difference between being broke and confused versus being clear and in control. Once you start seeing your money clearly, you can finally start directing it toward your freedom number.

What is Your Freedom Number?

Your freedom number is the monthly amount of passive income you need to live your ideal life without having to actively work for it.

Think of it as your "work optional" number: the point where your passive income covers 100 percent of your living expenses, lifestyle choices, and goals.

When you know this number, you no longer have to guess whether or not you're "on track." You can measure every decision, every investment, and every step you take against it.

Why it Matters

Without a target, even good financial habits feel aimless. You might save, invest here and there, or pay down debt, but you'll never know when you've "made it."

When you know your freedom number, you gain:

- **Clarity** – A specific, measurable goal.

- **Motivation** – A reason to keep going when it gets difficult.

- **Direction** – A filter for every financial decision.

How to Calculate Your Freedom Number

Here's a simple formula to get started:

1. Add up your current monthly expenses.

This includes your mortgage or rent, utilities, food, insurance, car costs, subscriptions, and any other regular bills. Don't forget the small stuff; it adds up fast.

2. Add the cost of your desired lifestyle upgrades.

Think about what your ideal life looks like. New car? Private school for your children? A second home? Maybe you want to take your family to Europe every year. Add those additional costs.

3. Factor in long-term goals and giving.

This could include investing in future projects, charitable giving, or helping family.

4. Multiply by twelve to get the annual number.

This is how much annual passive income you need to be fully free.

Example:

- Current expenses = $5,000/month

- Lifestyle upgrades = $2,000/month

- Long-term goals = $1,000/month

- **Total = $8,000/month → $96,000/year**

That's your freedom number.

For most people, it falls between $5,000–$10,000 per month, but it's different for everyone. Maybe you want to live frugally while traveling the world like my wife and me, or maybe you dream of a beachfront home and full-time family adventures. Either way, your lifestyle has a cost.

Budgeting gives you the data to determine what that cost is and how close you are to achieving it.

"A budget is telling your money where to go instead of wondering where it went." – John Maxwell

Our Monthly Ritual

For the past few years, Amanda and I have maintained an hour-long monthly ritual that keeps us aligned and financially focused.

We open our bank and credit card statements. We pull up our budget tracking spreadsheet and input every single transaction from the past month. I'm talking about groceries, gas, subscriptions, restaurants, gifts, Amazon purchases (yeah, that rabbit hole)—everything. If it costs us money, it goes on the spreadsheet.

We track what we:

- Earned

- Spent

- Saved

- Invested

- Gave

This simple practice helps us spot the leaks. It shows us when a category is creeping up. It reminds us to cancel unused subscriptions, and it gets us talking—not arguing—about our goals and what matters most.

This one habit has saved us thousands of dollars, prevented countless arguments, and given us complete confidence in our financial game plan. Plus, if you have children, you know how rare it is to sit down for an uninterrupted hour with your spouse to actually discuss life.

Plugging the Leaks

When you don't track your money, you don't just waste it; you lose the ability to optimize it.

Most people stay stuck pouring money into buckets riddled with holes. No matter how much they earn, it keeps draining out. A consistent budget is how you plug the holes.

Let's say you discover you're spending $700 a month eating out. That's not good or bad; it's just data. Now you can decide: Is this aligned with our goals? Could we reduce that to $300 and redirect the other $400 to build savings, pay off debt, or invest to create passive income?

This is what we call cash flow recovery, the first step in our Legacy Lifestyle Process. Before you can grow or protect wealth, you have to reclaim it. Budgeting is where that starts.

Systems Beat Willpower

You are exactly where you are because of the systems and habits you've maintained up until this point. Not your goals. Not your income. Not your upbringing. Your systems.

That truth can be hard to swallow, but it's liberating once you do, because systems can be changed.

Want to save more? Track your spending.

Want to invest more? Automate your transfers.

Want to spend less? Remove temptation. Unsubscribe from those emails. Delete the apps.

Habits aren't about motivation; they're about design. We don't budget because we have superhuman discipline. We budget because we built a system that makes it manageable.

A Simple Budgeting System to Start Today

If you're new to budgeting, keep it simple.

Start with four categories:

Bucket 1: Essentials (Fixed Spending)

This bucket holds money for necessary, recurring expenses such as rent or mortgage payments, utility bills, groceries, and debt payments. It should contain enough to cover all predictable costs until your next payday. Automating transfers to this account is recommended.

Bucket 2: Lifestyle (Flexible Spending)

This is your "fun money" bucket for variable and non-essential expenses. This includes discretionary spending like dining out, entertainment, hobbies, and shopping. Limiting yourself to only the funds in this bucket helps prevent overspending on wants.

Bucket 3: Short-Term Savings (Sinking Funds)

This bucket is for larger, planned expenses that occur periodically, so you don't have to scramble when they arise. Examples include annual car insurance premiums, starting your family trust, vacation savings, or a new phone. The goal is to save a little each month so the full amount is available when needed. Later in the book, I'll tell you exactly where you should keep this money so it's never not working for you.

Bucket 4: Freedom Fund (Wealth Building)

This bucket is dedicated to your financial goals: investing, building passive income, education funds, and emergency savings. These funds are typically invested in different asset categories that provide consistent cash flow. This bucket is where your future wealth grows.

Track your spending in each bucket for thirty days. Don't judge; just collect the data. After that, make adjustments that reflect your goals.

There are dozens of great tools available, such as You Need A Budget (YNAB), EveryDollar, Mint, or a basic budget template in Google Sheets. The tool doesn't matter; the consistency does.

When you align your income with these four categories, something powerful happens:

- You stop overspending on things that don't move you forward.

- You start saving with purpose.

- You stop feeling guilty about fun because you planned for it.

- You begin building not just wealth, but a rich life.

Ask yourself this simple question every time you feel the urge to spend money on something that isn't completely necessary: How does this move me closer to my goal?

At the end of the day, you're in control. You make the decisions, and you determine the results. What more could you ask for?

Real-World Example: The $80K Transformation

Marcus and Alana, a couple I worked with, earned $80,000 a year. That's plenty to build momentum, yet they constantly felt like they were behind.

Here's what we discovered:

- $700/month was going to dining out, random shopping, and unused subscriptions.

- They had no emergency savings.

- They had $24,000 in credit card debt.

- They had no real investment strategy.

- They had zero allocation for growth or legacy.

They weren't failing; they were just misaligned.

Here's what we changed:

- We rebuilt their spending plan using the Four-Bucket system.

- We set up automatic transfers to separate accounts for future growth and opportunities.

- We paid off debt using the snowball method while building savings at the same time (we'll talk about this more in the next chapter).

- We redirected their Freedom Fund toward sound investments.

Within eighteen months, they:

- Eliminated $24,000 in bad debt.

- Saved $7,000 in their Freedom Fund.

- Started building capital for their first private lending opportunity.

- Took a guilt-free family vacation they paid for with their own family banking system.

Same income. Completely different outcome. That's the power of having a system.

Your Action Plan:
Build Your Four-Bucket Budget

1. List your total monthly income (after taxes).

2. Allocate it across the four buckets (start with rough estimates; you can adjust later).

3. Identify where you're underfunding key categories (especially your Freedom Fund).

4. Open subaccounts for each bucket (you can have multiple checking/savings accounts with one bank).

5. Automate transfers so the system works even on your off days.

Remember: Automation beats discipline when it comes to money.

The Bottom Line

I know that budgeting isn't the sexiest part of wealth-building. It's not flashy, and it won't go viral on social media, but it is foundational to your success. It's how you get clear on your present so you can build the future you actually want. It's how you recover your cash flow and redirect it into your private family banking system, and it's how you move from being reactive with your money to being strategic with it.

It doesn't have to be perfect, but you do have to start. The earlier you build this habit, the faster everything else in this book will fall into place.

In the next chapter, we'll address something that might be holding you back from implementing any wealth-building strategy: DEBT. If you're currently carrying debt, don't worry, you haven't failed, you're not behind, and you're definitely not alone. I'll show you exactly how to break free from those chains so you can focus on building the life you want.

Consider downloading our free, easy-to-use budget template to get started tracking your cash flow today (https://legacylifeprocess.com/budget-template-and-training).

CHAPTER 3

Breaking Free from Debt

Debt is the thief of your future, but it doesn't have to be your destiny.

Now that you understand what success means to you and have a system to control your cash flow, we need to address the elephant in the room that might be keeping you from building wealth: DEBT.

Debt can be a real pain in the ass—believe me, I know. A few years ago, my wife and I were carrying a decent chunk of it ourselves. It wasn't anything crazy, but for regular working people like us, we felt its weight hovering over us constantly. Together, we had nearly $60,000 in debt, about $40,000 in student loans with my name on it, and the rest in high-interest credit cards that had quietly crept up to around $20,000.

Like so many others, we weren't reckless spenders. We were just doing what we thought we were supposed to do: go to school, get good jobs, try to build credit by using the cards when "needed," always make the minimum payments plus a little extra. Rinse and repeat.

But here's the deal: Life happens, and we realized we couldn't build the future we wanted if all we were doing was paying for our past.

We knew something had to change, not just for us, but for the family we were building. By implementing some of the tools and processes we'll discuss throughout this book, in just over a year, we eliminated every dollar we had in debt while still allowing our $60,000 to work for us in our private banking system, earning and growing.

This chapter isn't about bragging; it's about hope. It's about possibility, because I want you to know that if regular people like us can do it, you absolutely can too.

Welcome to America's Debt Nightmare

Let's zoom out for a second. This isn't just a "you" problem or a "me" problem. This is a full-blown American crisis, and it's getting worse every year.

Get this:

- The average American household carries over $100,000 in total debt.

- Forty-five million people are still paying off student loans (some of them well into their fifties and sixties).

- The average credit card APR is now over 20 percent. That's borderline criminal, if you ask me.

Debt has become the norm, and that's the real problem here.

We're taught to live beyond our means from day one. Everyone's constantly trying to keep up with the Joneses (or these days, the

Kardashians). Credit gets handed out like candy, especially to young adults entering college. We all know the information we actually need is nowhere to be found in a classroom, but that doesn't mean you have to be a victim of this system. It just means you've got to be willing to take the time to educate yourself. A mentor once said to me: Don't let your schooling interfere with your education.

Our Personal Breakthrough Moment

What changed everything for us wasn't some magical mindset shift; it was getting educated and building the right system.

We found mentors. We got serious about our cash flow, which meant actually creating and sticking to a budget (I know, budgets aren't sexy, but they work). We started using what I now know to be some pretty sophisticated financial strategies. There's a strong possibility that the tool we were taught to use and the way we were taught to use it will feel like a completely foreign concept. Don't worry, as the book goes on, I'll explain exactly why this is considered to be the toughest asset out there for storing, growing, and leveraging wealth. Here's what our plan looked like:

- Putting our savings and any extra money we could scrape together into a properly structured, dividend-paying whole life policy from a mutual company (aka our family banking system).

- Using the funds immediately available within the policy to take a loan against and pay down our debts (essentially turning outside debt, the third-party lenders controlled, into inside debt we controlled).

- Because we first flowed our money into our properly structured family banking system, we were able to earn uninterrupted compounding growth on our dollars while simultaneously leveraging them to eliminate debt. Don't worry, I'll explain this in detail as we get into future chapters.

- After each debt was paid off, we would redirect the monthly payments we were making to third-party creditors back to ourselves as a policy loan repayment, which allowed us to recapture the interest that otherwise would have escaped our system and put those dollars back to work paying down the next debt on our list.

It was like flipping a switch. Instead of feeling trapped, we started feeling in control. Debt no longer had a grip on us because we finally had a system that actually worked.

The moment we saw that first credit card hit a zero balance we were ecstatic . We knew it worked. Now we just had to stick to it. One by one, the debts started falling. Then finally, the student debt was gone.

I still remember paying off the last chunk of my student loans. I can't begin to tell you what it felt like to have that weight lifted off my shoulders, and the best part was that I was still earning on every penny of that $40,000 I sent to Sallie Mae, all thanks to the specially designed whole life policy we built to become our family banking system. Even as I write this, it's a damn good feeling to think back on. I want you to experience that same feeling.

From Stuck to Strategic

Here's what I've learned: Too many people believe they're just stuck. They think debt is simply part of life in America. They assume their paycheck will never stretch far enough, and they've convinced themselves that building real wealth just isn't in the cards for regular folks like us.

But let me be crystal clear about something: **You don't need to be wealthy to get started, but you do need to get started to become wealthy.**

Debt doesn't disqualify you from building wealth; it just means you need a better plan. A plan built on clarity, consistency, systems, and support.

If you're reading this and you're currently buried in debt, listen to me for a second: You haven't failed, you're not behind, and you are definitely not alone. You don't need to feel ashamed, but you do need a new path. As someone who's been exactly where you are, I feel like it's my responsibility to help you find it.

Whether you've got $5,000 or $500,000 worth of debt hanging over your head, with the right plan in place, you can eliminate all of it. I know that for a fact because the same system that helped us get out of debt is the one I've taught to countless others, helping them move from survival mode to building a life of actual freedom. When I work with people now, I don't just help them "budget better" (though budgeting is important). I help them completely restructure how their money flows. I use specific tools and systems to show them how to create breathing room, and walk them through redirecting those debt payments into wealth-building systems so they can eliminate debt faster than they thought possible.

Amanda's and my biggest problem early on was that we didn't have a concrete plan. Once we started working with people who stressed the importance of systematic budgeting and debt elimination, everything changed. They helped us create a real plan with a clear timeline, showing us exactly how to pay off our debts one by one, and when we'd finally be free from all the shit that was holding us down.

The Debt Snowball: Your Best Friend

If you're just starting your debt elimination journey, I'm going to introduce you to what might become your new best friend: the debt snowball method.

For most people, this approach works like magic. You list your debts from smallest balance to largest (ignore interest rates for now, we'll talk about why in a minute) and knock them out one by one while reallocating every dollar from a paid-off debt toward the next debt in line. This creates massive momentum.

This method not only helps you rack up quick psychological wins, but it also accelerates your payoff timeline in one of the most efficient ways possible. There are other approaches out there, but if you're looking to tackle this on your own and need some quick wins, the snowball method is hands down the best place to start.

Here's exactly how it works:

Step 1: List all your debts from smallest balance to largest (seriously, ignore those interest rates for now).

Step 2: Make minimum payments on all debts except the smallest one.

Step 3: Attack that smallest debt with every extra dollar you can find. I'm talking about spare change from your car, money from selling stuff you don't need, side hustle income—whatever you can get your hands on.

Step 4: Once that smallest debt is eliminated, take that entire payment amount and add it to the minimum payment of the next smallest debt.

Step 5: Repeat this process until every single debt you have is paid off.

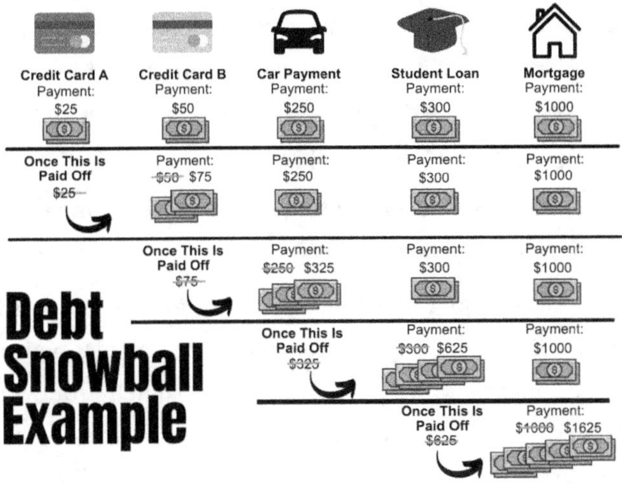

The key here is discipline. When you're paying off debts one by one, don't you dare look at that newly freed-up cash as extra spending money. That's fuel for your ever-growing snowball. This extra cash flow is going to give you the momentum you need to eliminate debt faster than you ever thought possible.

Now, you might be wondering: Why ignore the interest rates? Wouldn't it be smarter to pay off the highest interest debt first?

Mathematically, yes, you'd end up saving a few bucks. But here's the thing, this isn't just about math; it's about psychology. When you pay off that first small debt, you get a win. When you pay off the second one, you get another win. Those wins build confidence, and confidence builds momentum, and momentum is what's going to carry you through the tough months when you want to quit. Trust me on this one.

The Question That Changed Everything for Me

As I was going through this exact process, I developed what became the most helpful habit of my financial life. Anytime I felt the urge to spend money I either didn't have or would have to put on a credit card, I'd ask myself one simple question:

How does this move me closer to my goal of becoming debt-free and going *From Regular to Rich*?

Let me be clear about something: Nobody's asking you to give up the things you enjoy forever. But if you're just a regular person like me, you're going to need some serious financial help from yourself to kickstart this journey. The dollars you save in these moments over the next few years could be exactly what you need to fuel your financial fire.

At the end of the day, you're in control. You make the decisions. You determine the results. The sooner you start, the faster your snowball builds momentum.

Beyond Basic: Advanced Debt Elimination

Once you understand the fundamentals, there are some more sophisticated approaches that can turbocharge the whole process. These strategies allow you to:

- Pay off debt while keeping your money growing elsewhere.

- Maintain liquidity for emergencies or opportunities that pop up.

- Actually recapture the interest you would have paid to creditors.

- Build wealth at the same time you're eliminating debt.

Now, these strategies involve some specialized financial products and should definitely be implemented with guidance from professionals who understand both debt elimination and wealth-building principles inside and out. But the key insight I want you to get is this: You don't have to choose between paying off debt and building wealth. With the right system, you can absolutely do both at the same time.

The Plot Twist: From Debt Payments to Wealth Building

Here's something most people don't realize: The same principles that help you eliminate debt efficiently can be used to build wealth effectively. The discipline you develop, the systems you create, and the mindset you cultivate during debt elimination become the foundation for everything that comes next.

In fact, people who successfully eliminate debt often become the absolute best wealth builders because they've already learned:

- How to live below their means without feeling deprived.

- The power of systematic, consistent approaches.

- The importance of delayed gratification (which is huge).

- How to make money work harder than they do.

Once you're debt-free, those monthly payments you were making don't just disappear; they become your wealth-building ammunition. Instead of sending money to creditors every month, you get to redirect all that cash flow toward assets that actually pay you back.

This is where the real magic happens, and it's exactly what we'll dive into throughout the rest of this book.

Time to Take Action

The most important step is always the first one. Whether you decide to go with the simple snowball method or eventually explore some of the more advanced strategies, the key is just to begin.

Start by:

1. Listing every single debt you have with balances and minimum payments.

2. Choosing your elimination strategy (snowball method is the most beginner-friendly).

3. Finding extra money in your budget to accelerate those payments (yes, that means cutting things that aren't moving you closer to your goal or picking up extra work).

4. Celebrating the small wins as each debt disappears, not by spending more money but spending more time with the people you love (this is important—give yourself credit).

5. Planning what you're going to do with those payments once you're debt-free.

Remember: Every dollar you're sending to creditors today is a dollar that won't be building your wealth tomorrow. The faster you eliminate debt, the sooner you can redirect that cash flow toward building the rich life you defined back in Chapter 1.

If you need help putting together a more sophisticated plan, there are qualified professionals like myself out there who specialize in debt elimination and wealth-building strategies. Just make sure you're working with someone who actually understands both sides of the equation.

The bottom line? You've got this. It might take some time, it's definitely going to require some discipline, but you absolutely have what it takes to get this done.

In our next chapter, we're going to talk about something that's going to make everything else easier: building the habits that create lasting wealth. Because once you've got your debt handled and you understand how to control your cash flow, the habits you develop will determine whether you stay financially free or slip back into old patterns.

Let's make sure you stay free.

CHAPTER 4

The Habits That Build a Rich Life

Why Habits Come Before Wealth

Before we dive deep into the world of wealth-building strategies, legacy planning, and private banking, we need to start with something far more foundational: your habits.

This chapter is inspired by one of the most impactful books I've ever read: *Atomic Habits* by James Clear. If you truly want to master your behavior, create better systems, live intentionally, and give yourself the best chance of going *From Regular to Rich*, read that book cover to cover. I cannot recommend it enough.

What I'll share here are the lessons that had the biggest impact on me, because let's be honest: Wealth doesn't just come from a decent investing strategy. It comes from consistency. And consistency is built on habits.

Lesson 1: Why Habits Matter More Than Goals

We've all been told to set goals. Create a vision board. Chase the dream. Manifest your destiny. All that stuff. The problem is that goals are useless without systems.

James Clear puts it perfectly: "You do not rise to the level of your goals. You fall to the level of your systems." Think about it. Every Olympian, entrepreneur, and millionaire had the same goal as their competitors: to win the race, build the business, and become financially free, but not all of them made it. What separated the winners wasn't the goal; they all had that. It was the system behind the scenes, the daily habits shaping their actions. If your goal is financial independence but your daily habit is scrolling Amazon and impulse-buying random stuff, your system is working against you. Your current life is the result of your current habits. Not your hopes. Not your plans. Your habits.

That can be a tough pill to swallow, but here's the silver lining: If habits got you here, then new habits can take you somewhere better.

Lesson 2: The Power of Tiny Gains

One of the most memorable ideas from *Atomic Habits* is this: "If you get 1% better every day for a year, you'll end up 37 times better by the end of the year." That's compound growth, but applied to your behavior.

We'll talk plenty about how money compounds throughout this book, but the same principle applies to habits. You don't have to overhaul your entire life in a weekend; you just need to get 1 percent better. Then another percent. Then another. That could look like:

- Waking up ten minutes earlier.

- Reviewing your budget for five minutes.

- Skipping one drive-thru per week.

- Reading ten pages of a financial book each day.

Small wins, stacked over time, create massive outcomes. The magic isn't in the individual action; it's in the compounding effect of consistency.

Lesson 3: The Diderot Effect (and the Habits That Hurt)

There's a trap most people (including myself for years) don't even notice. It's called the Diderot Effect, and the idea is simple: One new purchase can trigger a wave of unnecessary spending.

The term comes from Denis Diderot, a French philosopher who was once gifted a luxurious robe by Catherine the Great. Once he owned it, all his other belongings suddenly looked cheap and unworthy. So he replaced everything—the rug, the chair, the art—with more elegant pieces, and in the process, he went broke.

We still do this today.

- You get a new pair of shoes. → Suddenly you "need" a whole new outfit.

- You get a raise. → Suddenly you "need" a nicer car.

- You buy a new house. → Now you "need" new furniture for every room.

- You have a wedding or a baby. → Suddenly everything "needs" to be upgraded.

It's not just lifestyle creep; it's habit creep. One small purchase triggers another, then another. Before you know it, you've built an entire system of habits that are quietly draining your financial future.

Lesson 4: Identity-Based Habits and Redefining Yourself

One of the most profound lessons James Clear teaches is the idea of identity-based habits. Instead of focusing on what you want to achieve, focus on who you want to become.

- Want to build wealth? Start saying: "I am a disciplined investor."

- Want to be healthy? Start saying: "I am the kind of person who takes care of their body."

- Want to be debt-free? Start saying: "I am someone who makes smart financial decisions."

When you believe something about yourself, your habits naturally align with that belief. But here's the crazy part; the reverse is true too. If you keep telling yourself "I'm bad with money" or "I'll never be wealthy," you'll find ways to live that out. Your behavior will sabotage your progress because your habits stay consistent with your identity.

This book isn't just about becoming "rich"; it's about becoming someone who lives richly, acts with intention, and builds a system of habits that serve them instead of sabotage them.

Lesson 5: The Stonecutter's Persistence

There's a quote in the book that James Clear refers to from Jacob Riis that I believe does a great job capturing the spirit of building wealth and habits over time:

When nothing seems to help, I go and look at a stonecutter hammering away at his rock perhaps a hundred times without as much as a crack showing in it. Yet at the hundred and first blow, it will split in two, and I know it was not that last blow that did it, but all that had gone before.

That's the habit mindset. You may not see results today. You may not feel the progress tomorrow. But every time you choose the right action, you're hitting the stone. Every habit is another swing of the hammer. Eventually, the stone will break open.

Wealth Habits That Actually Move the Needle

All right, let's get practical. Here are the specific habits that I've seen make the biggest difference in people's financial lives:

Weekly Money Date (thirty minutes)

Every week, sit down and review your spending. Are you on track with your budget? Any surprises? Any adjustments needed? This prevents small problems from becoming big ones.

Monthly Financial Review (sixty minutes)

This is the deep dive. Review your entire financial picture. How much did you save? How much did you invest? What worked? What didn't? This is where you make strategic adjustments.

Daily Learning (fifteen minutes)

Read something about money, investing, or personal development every single day. It could be a chapter, an article, a podcast episode—it doesn't matter. The key is consistency.

Automate Everything

Automate your savings, investments, and bill payments. Remove the need for daily financial decisions. When good financial behavior happens automatically, you can't mess it up.

The "Hell Yes" or "No" Rule

One habit that's been a game-changer for me is before making any non-essential purchase, I ask myself a simple question: Is this a hell yes?

If it's not an immediate, enthusiastic "hell yes," then it's a no.

For example:

- Do I need the new shoes, or are my current shoes just fine?

- Is the newest iPhone 100 percent necessary, or does the one I currently have still get the job done?

- Does my kid really need all these toys for Christmas he'll probably never really play with, or would I rather get him just a few things I know he would love?

- I have a vacation coming up. Do I really need a bunch of new outfits just for the occasion, or does my current wardrobe get the job done?

This simple filter has saved me thousands of dollars on stuff I thought I wanted but didn't actually need. It forces you to be intentional about your spending instead of reactive.

Make Habits the Wealth Strategy

Here's what I want you to take away from this chapter:

- You are not your circumstances. You are your systems.

- Your current results were created by your current habits.
- Your future can be shaped by the new habits you choose today.

Forget motivation. That comes and goes. Forget willpower. That gets depleted. Build systems that work even when you don't feel like it.

Start with 1 percent. Stack your wins. Watch what happens over time.

Then go read *Atomic Habits*. Highlight every other page. Re-read it every year. Keep hammering that stone.

Because eventually, it's going to crack.

The Truth Nobody Wants to Say Out Loud

Before we move on, let's get real for a second.

You can build the best habits in the world. You can read every book, follow every guru, and track every dollar, and yes, that will absolutely change your life for the better.

But it won't change the game you've been forced to play.

You're working your ass off to get ahead, but the system? It's designed to pull you back down, to keep you ordinary. Just enough comfort to keep you quiet. Just enough struggle to keep you tired and distracted.

They don't want you thinking too deeply about where your money goes.

They don't want you asking why your taxes rise while your paycheck stays the same.

They don't want you to realize that banks, Wall Street, and the government are all playing a completely different game than you are.

No, they want you busy, distracted, and chasing goals without ever gaining any real ground. But here's the thing: You're different now. You've started building the right habits. You've started thinking bigger. You're waking up to what's really going on, and once you wake up, you can't unsee the truth.

That's where we're heading next. In Chapter 5 , we'll pull back the curtain on the institutions that have quietly kept everyday people financially stuck for generations. Not out of spite or because they hate you, but because that's how the system was designed to work.

The good news is that once you know what's going on, you'll know what to do.

Why Traditional Systems Fall Short

You're not behind because you're lazy. You're behind because nobody taught you how money actually works.

By now, you've built your foundation: You know what success means to you, you've gotten control of your cash flow, you've tackled your debt, and you're creating wealth-building habits.

Here's what we need to address now: If following the traditional financial advice actually worked, you wouldn't need this book. You'd see families around you thriving financially. Your parents would be living comfortably in retirement. Your friends would be stress-free about money. The "work hard, save in a 401(k), retire at sixty-five" formula would be creating financial freedom everywhere you looked.

Instead, consider where the traditional system has gotten us:

- **Sixty percent of Americans live paycheck to paycheck** (LendingClub 2024)—and that includes people earning six figures.[3]

- **Only 37 percent of people feel on track for retirement** (Federal Reserve 2023).[4]

- **Seventy-seven percent of Americans are anxious about their finances** (APA Stress in America Report 2024).[5]

- **Average household debt is at all-time highs**, with credit card balances alone passing $1.1 trillion in 2024.[6]

These aren't lazy people. These aren't people who don't try. These are hardworking Americans following what little financial advice they were given.

The system isn't broken. It's working exactly as designed—it just wasn't designed for you.

Meet Sarah and Mike

Sarah and Mike did everything "right." For thirty years, Mike maxed out his 401(k) at the manufacturing plant while Sarah contributed to her teacher's retirement plan. They saved diligently, lived below their means, and followed every piece of conventional financial wisdom.

---

3   LendingClub Corporation and PYMNTS. *"New Reality Check: Paycheck-to-Paycheck Report."* January 2024. https://www.pymnts.com

4   Board of Governors of the Federal Reserve System. *"Economic Well-Being of U.S. Households in 2023."* May 2024. https://www.federalreserve.gov/consumerscommunities/shed.htm

5   American Psychological Association. *"Stress in America 2024: The State of Our Nation."* October 2024. https://www.apa.org/news/press/releases/stress

6   Federal Reserve Bank of New York. *"Household Debt and Credit Report, Q2 2024."* August 2024. https://www.newyorkfed.org/microeconomics/hhdc.html

In 2007, at age fifty-five, they had accumulated $850,000 in their retirement accounts. They were on track for a comfortable retirement at sixty-five.

Then 2008 hit. Their accounts dropped to $425,000—half their life savings were gone in months. While the market eventually recovered, they were forced to keep working five extra years to make up the losses. Mike's health declined during those extra working years, and he passed away at sixty-seven, just two years into retirement.

Sarah, now sixty-nine, lives on $2,800 per month from their diminished accounts, plus Social Security. The "guaranteed" teacher's pension was underfunded and cut benefits by 30 percent. She now works part-time at a grocery store to make ends meet.

Sarah followed the rules. She trusted the system. She did everything the "experts" told her to do. Yet she's working at sixty-nine while watching her savings slowly drain away.

This isn't a story about bad luck. This is the logical outcome of a system that transfers all risk to you while promising security it can't deliver.

The Three Core Problems

Problem 1: Your Financial Education Was Incomplete

"It's not how much money you make. It's how much money you keep." - Robert Kiyosaki

Think back to school. You memorized state capitals, the periodic table, and were taught all about the Revolutionary War, but when did anyone teach you:

- How compound interest really works?
- The difference between assets and liabilities?

- How taxes actually affect your wealth building?

- What inflation does to your purchasing power?

- How banks profit from your deposits?

They didn't, because if everyone understood how money truly flows, fewer people would hand over control of their financial future to institutions designed to profit from their ignorance.

Problem 2: Traditional Retirement Accounts Transfer Risk to You

Here's what happened: In the 1970s and '80s, companies started replacing guaranteed pensions with 401(k)s because pensions became a significant, unpredictable financial liability for the employers who had to fund and manage them. Pension plans, which are considered to be "defined benefit" plans, guarantee a specific monthly payment in retirement, creating a long-term, potentially rising financial liability for the employer. 401(k)s, or "defined contribution" plans, were far less expensive because the employer's responsibility was limited to at most matching contributions of their employees instead of guaranteeing a final payout. This wasn't a gift to employees—it was a way for corporations to transfer retirement risk from the company to you.

Now *YOU* bear all the risk:

- Market crashes? Your problem.

- Inflation eating your purchasing power? Your problem.

- Rising tax rates in retirement? Your problem.

- Fees compounding against you year after year? You guessed it, your problem.

When you choose tax-deferred vehicles like 401(k)s and IRAs, you're taking on two specific risks that most people never consider:

1. The Unknown

When it comes to taxes, there are two key variables you can't control: the tax rate when you withdraw and the tax bracket you're in when you pay.

Most people assume they'll be in a lower bracket in retirement because they'll no longer be receiving the same income they once did during their working years. My question is: Why plan your life around earning less? When you invest in a tax-deferred vehicle, you're giving up control to the individual or company making the investments for you. You don't know what your future tax rate will be, what your tax bracket will be, or what the rules will look like ten, twenty, or thirty years from now.

Currently, at age seventy-three, Required Minimum Distributions (RMDs) kick in. That means even if you don't need the money sitting in your qualified plan, the government forces you to take it out and pay taxes at whatever rate exists at that time. Say you're bringing in good income from the passive investments you've made over time. Let's also assume that said income is $200,000 a year, which puts you right at the top of the 2025 federal tax rate for someone paying 24 percent. Now that you're seventy-three and the government is forcing you to take withdrawals from your qualified plan, you pass that $201,775 a year threshold for the 24 percent tax bracket, and now you will be forced to pay a 32 percent tax on all the additional income you're having to pull from your 401(k) or IRA, even though it's not something you need to live on. I also want you to understand that the 32 percent bracket I mentioned is not the top tax bracket, nor is it the amount you're guaranteed to pay in twenty or thirty years from now when you officially reach the age of Required Minimum Distributions.

2. The Gamble

People choose tax deferral because they believe their taxes will be lower in retirement. Think about what that really means: "I believe I'll be poorer in the future."

If your plan is to hopefully earn less so you can pay less in taxes, that's not financial freedom—that's planning for defeat. Plus, income from tax-deferred plans is treated as earned income. That means it's taxed at even higher rates than capital gains or dividends. In my experience, many retirees discover their retirement withdrawals are taxed more heavily than expected.

Imagine you're a farmer with a single truckload of seed to plant today. After a full growing season, you expect to harvest ten truckloads. Now you have a choice:

- Pay a known tax on the seed today.

- Pay an unknown tax on the entire harvest later.

If you're thinking like a wealth builder, you pay the tax on the seed today. It's smaller, predictable, and easier to manage. You're protecting your harvest.

With tax-deferred plans like the 401(k), the 403(b), the IRA, and many others, you're choosing to pay tax on the harvest. You're betting that you'll get a better deal later, but the opposite often happens. You pay more because you're taxing a larger amount at an unknown future rate. We are currently in what's considered to be one of the lower historic tax-rate environments for the U.S., particularly when comparing to past decades. Betting that taxes will stay this low is a gamble that could end up costing you a massive chunk of your retirement. I'm not a huge fan of qualified plans in general, but if you are going to invest your money using those types of plans to set yourself up for retirement, my focus would be on anything that allows me to pay the taxes now and pull out tax free cash later. For example, the Roth 401(k) or Roth IRA.

The Average vs. Actual Problem

Financial advisors love talking about "average returns" when it comes to the market. Somehow using a specific set of data, they'll convince you that your 401(k) or IRA should average about 8 to 10 percent a year over an extended period of time, but average isn't actual. Here's why this matters:

Year	Return	Balance
1	50%	$100,000 → $150,000
2	-50%	$150,000 → $75,000
3	50%	$75,000 → $112,500
4	-50%	$112,500 → $56,250
Average Return = 0%		
Actual Return = -43.75%		

The "average" return is 0 percent, but you actually lost 43.75 percent of your money. This is the difference between average returns (what they show you in brochures) and actual returns (what happens to your money).

The Hidden Drag of Fees and Taxes

One thing people often overlook when taking part in a qualified plan like the ones mentioned above and handing their money over to someone else to manage is the *cost* of that convenience—the fees. If someone other than you is managing your investments, it's worth asking what percentage they're actually charging in total fees. Because even a small number can make a big difference over time.

For example, let's look at what a seemingly minor 2 percent annual fee on a $100,000 investment earning 10 percent really costs over thirty years:

Scenario	Annual Return	Balance After 30 Years
No Fees	10%	$1,744,940
2% Fee	8%	$1,006,266
Cost of 2% Fee - $738,674 (42% less)		

That 2 percent fee didn't cost you 2 percent—it cost you 42 percent of your potential wealth. When you add taxes on top of fees, the erosion becomes even more severe.

The Martinez Family Discovery

When Mr. Martinez finally sat down to analyze his 401(k) after fifteen years of contributions, he was shocked. His statements showed "average annual returns" of 8 percent, but his actual account value told a different story.

He'd contributed $180,000 over fifteen years. With 8 percent returns, he should have had roughly $390,000. Instead, his account showed $310,000.

Where did the $80,000 go?

His financial advisor helped him trace it:

- Management fees: $45,000.

- Administrative fees: $18,000.

- Lost opportunity during market downturns: $17,000.

He realized he'd been paying nearly $5,500 per year in fees—money that could have been compounding for his family instead of funding someone else's profits. Even worse, those fees came out whether his account went up or down.

"I felt like I'd been working two jobs," Mr. Martinez told me. "One for my family, and one for Wall Street."

When Mr. Martinez and I started working together, we took a different approach. Instead of continuing to feed a system that profited more from his money than he did, we redirected his savings into a properly structured whole life policy, creating his own private banking system, and paired it with a deferred income annuity (provides guaranteed income for life) to create predictable, guaranteed income for the future. Now, his dollars are compounding uninterrupted, and when he needs access to cash, he can borrow against his own policy instead of draining his savings or relying on the market.

Within the first year, he told me the biggest difference wasn't just in his numbers; it was in how he felt. For the first time, Mr. Martinez said he finally understood where his money was going and what it was doing for him. The stress was gone. The control was back in his hands. His plan now includes growth, liquidity, and long-term income—all working together to build real financial security for his family, not for someone else's balance sheet.

Problem 3: Traditional Banks Use Your Money Against You

When you put money in a savings account, you think you're being responsible. The bank sees it differently: Your deposit is their raw material.

Here's how it works:

- You deposit $10,000; they pay you 0.05 percent ($5 per year).

- They immediately lend that money out at 6 to 20 percent interest.

- Your $10,000 earns them $600 to $2,000 while costing them $5.

- They keep the spread; you keep the risk of inflation eating your purchasing power.

Let's run the numbers on what this really costs you. Say you keep $50,000 in a traditional savings account for ten years, earning 0.05 percent interest:

- After ten years, you'll have made around $250 in interest.

Now imagine the same money earning a modest 4 percent annually, compounded:

- After ten years, you'd have $74,012.

- That's a $23,762 difference.

This isn't theoretical—this is the real cost of letting banks use your money instead of putting it to work for yourself. Every dollar sitting in traditional savings is a dollar that isn't building your wealth.

Old School vs. Private Banking System

Banks don't build wealth by owning money—they build wealth by controlling the flow of money. The question is: Why let them control yours when you can control it yourself?

Traditional Approach	Properly Structured Whole Life
Savings account (0.05% return)	Guaranteed 4-5% growth
Term life + invest the difference	Permanent protection + cash growth
Emergency fund (little to no growth)	Accessible cash that compounds
Taxable investments	Tax-advantaged accumulation
No borrowing power	Asset-backed lending capability

"The rich don't save in banks, they own them." - Garrett Gunderson, *What Would the Rockefellers Do?*

While you're following the traditional rules, the wealthy operate by different principles:

- **They don't rely on one income stream**—they build multiple cash-flowing assets.

- **They don't give up control**—they maintain liquidity and access to their capital.

- **They don't defer taxes indefinitely**—they use current tax laws strategically.

- **They don't hope for market performance**—they create guaranteed growth with upside potential.

- **They don't just save money**—they put money to work earning returns while keeping it accessible.

Most importantly:

- **They don't follow the same rules they teach everyone else to follow.**

Why This Matters More Than Ever

The traditional financial advice was questionable in stable times. In today's economic environment, it's becoming dangerous.

Inflation is Back with a Vengeance

Your parents might remember when a Coke cost 25 cents. Today it's $2.50. That's not nostalgia—that's the hidden tax of inflation eating purchasing power. The Federal Reserve's money printing since 2008 has accelerated this trend. Your savings account earning 0.05

percent is losing 3 to 6 percent annually to inflation. You're going backward while thinking you're being responsible.

Market Volatility is the New Normal

The days of steady, predictable market growth are over. We've seen:

- The Dot-Com crash (2000–2002): 49 percent decline.
- The Financial Crisis (2007–2009): 57 percent decline.
- COVID Crash (2020): 34 percent decline in weeks.
- Recent volatility (2022): 25 percent decline.

If you're within ten to fifteen years of retirement, you don't have time to recover from the next crash. Yet, traditional advice keeps pushing you to "stay the course" while your timeline shrinks.

Tax Rates Are Going One Direction: Up

Federal debt is at historic highs. Social Security and Medicare are underfunded. State and local governments are struggling. The math is simple: Taxes have to go up. Yet traditional retirement accounts bet that your taxes will be lower in the future. That's not optimism— that's wishful thinking and poor planning.

The "Safe" Assets Aren't Safe Anymore

Bonds used to be the conservative choice. Today, with interest rates rising, bond portfolios are getting crushed. Real estate was the backup plan, but with mortgage rates doubling, that's becoming less accessible. Even Treasury bills—the "risk-free" investment—lose money after inflation and taxes.

The old playbook doesn't work in the new economy. You need strategies that were built for uncertainty, not ones that assume a stability that no longer exists.

I'm not sharing this to make you angry or paranoid. I'm sharing it so you understand why a different approach isn't just smart; it's necessary.

The financial services industry makes money whether your accounts go up or down. The government gets their taxes whether you're prepared or not. Traditional banks profit from your deposits whether you build wealth or don't . Your success is not their primary concern. It's yours.

There is an alternative approach that gives you:

- Guaranteed growth every year, regardless of market performance.

- Complete liquidity without penalties or restrictions.

- Tax advantages that work in your favor.

- Control over your money instead of handing it to institutions.

- The ability to use your money for multiple purposes simultaneously.

It's called becoming your own banker, and it's built on the same principles banks use to build wealth—except this time, you're in control. You can use specially structured life insurance policies, private lending, real estate partnerships, and business ownership to build wealth outside the traditional system.

Believe me, I get it. All of that can sound overwhelming if this is the first time you're ever hearing about it. Luckily, you don't have to wait until you understand every strategy to start taking back control. Here are three immediate actions that will begin shifting the momentum in your favor:

Step 1: Calculate Your Real Returns

Pull out your most recent 401(k) or IRA statement. Find your account value from exactly one year ago. Calculate your actual return—not what the market did, but what your account actually earned after fees. Compare that to what you contributed during the year. You might be surprised to find you've been working harder for your money than your money has for you.

Step 2: Track Your Opportunity Cost

Look at your savings and checking account balances. Calculate how much you're earning (probably close to zero) versus how much banks are making lending that same money out at 6 to 20 percent interest. Imagine if you were playing the role of the banker in this situation and earning that interest for yourself. This isn't about making you angry; it's about making you aware. Awareness is the first step toward better decisions.

Step 3: Question Every Financial "Rule"

For the next week, every time you hear traditional financial advice— from TV, friends, or even financial advisors—ask yourself: Who benefits if I follow this advice? Usually, it's not you. Start thinking like an owner instead of a customer. Owners ask different questions and make different choices.

These aren't huge moves, but they're the beginning of thinking differently about your money. Once you start seeing the system clearly, you can't unsee it. And once you can't unsee it, you'll be motivated to find a better way.

Moving Forward

This isn't about never using banks or avoiding all traditional investments. It's about building a foundation that works for you first, then strategically using other tools from a position of strength.

In the next chapter, we'll explore the Strategic Compounding Mindset—how to think about money growth in a way that protects your wealth while building it consistently, year after year, under your control.

The problems with traditional systems are real, but they don't have to define your financial future. You have the power to choose a different path.

It's time to try something different.

"The definition of insanity is doing the same thing over and over again and expecting different results." - Unknown

CHAPTER 6

The Strategic Compounding Mindset

By now, you've seen that traditional financial strategies are riddled with traps, high fees, delayed access, future taxes, and limited liquidity. If we're going to escape that system, we need more than a critique—we need a better model. That model begins with strategic compounding.

Most people say they understand compounding, but what they really understand is addition. They'll say things like: "If I save $500 a month, that's $6,000 a year. In ten years, I'll have $60,000." That's basic arithmetic, not compound growth.

Compound interest is exponential, and exponential math plays by completely different rules. One of the clearest ways to grasp it is through a famous thought experiment:

What would you rather have $1 million in cash right now, or a single penny that doubles every day for thirty days?

Most people would grab the million and run. Hell, to be honest, I was one of those people before I really understood the true power of uninterrupted compounding.

Here's what happens if you let that penny double:

Day	Amount	Day	Amount
1	$0.01	16	$327.68
2	$0.02	17	$655.36
3	$0.04	18	$1,310.72
4	$0.08	19	$2,621.44
5	$0.16	20	$5,242.88
6	$0.32	21	$10,485.76
7	$0.64	22	$20,971.52
8	$1.28	23	$41,943.04
9	$2.56	24	$83,886.08
10	$5.12	25	$167,772.16
11	$10.24	26	$335,544.32
12	$20.48	27	$671,088.64
13	$40.96	28	$1,342,177.28
14	$81.92	29	$2,684,354.56
15	$163.84	30	$5,368,709.12

That's right. A single penny, left alone to double daily for thirty days turns into over $5.3 million. But here's the critical part that most people miss: Compounding only works if it's uninterrupted.

The Real Cost of Interrupting Compounding

In the real world, your compounding gets interrupted constantly, by taxes, fees, market volatility, or unexpected circumstances that force you to spend. I get it, that's life, but to drive this point home, let's re-run the penny doubling scenario. This time, we'll introduce some real-world friction. Watch how fast the magic of compounding disappears.

Scenario 1: Fees

Let's say you're charged a **2 percent management fee**, something often considered "reasonable" in traditional financial circles.

Your ending balance drops from $5.3 million to **$2,988,313**. That's **over $2.3 million lost** to what appears on paper to be a "small" cost. This is what's happening inside millions of 401(k) and mutual fund accounts every single day. Silent, slow wealth erosion, barely noticed, never recovered.

Scenario 2: Use of Money

Now imagine you withdraw just $100 on day fifteen and another $100 on day twenty-five. That's $200 total out of your compounding machine. Your final balance is now **$2,088,709**.

Just two small withdrawals cost you **$3.2 million** in long-term growth. Not because of the amount spent, but because of the compounding potential that was lost forever. Every dollar spent is not just a dollar gone; it's a potential fortune erased.

Scenario 3: Losses

Now, let's say on days five, fifteen, and twenty-five, the penny doesn't double. Just three missed days out of thirty, but you still earn on the other days. That seems minor, right?

Instead of ending with $5.3 million, your final balance now comes out to just **$671,089**.

What's crazy is that technically on paper you only "lost" $42,025 because of the missed growth on those days, but since compounding builds on itself, the true opportunity cost was over **$4.6 million**.

Scenario 4: Taxes

Let's assume you're taxed at **15 percent** on all your gains. A modest rate by today's standards. Your final balance drops from $5.3 million down to **$559,732**.

You only paid **$182,736** in taxes, but lost **$4.8 million** in potential growth because of the compounding curve being flattened.

If taxes go up, the impact is even worse. This is why putting your money into tax-deferred accounts that delay the tax bill is such a risky gamble; you have no control over what the IRS will demand ten, twenty, or thirty years from now.

Scenario 5: All Four Combined

Now let's layer three of the four together, because in most cases all or most of these factors are affecting everyday people:

- You're charged a 2 percent fee.
- You miss your doubling on days five, fifteen, and twenty-five (losses).
- You pay a 15 percent tax.
- You decide not to withdraw (because you now understand the cost).

Your final balance is now **$51,368.** Compare that to the uninterrupted total of $5,368,709.

That's not a "small dip." That's a **99 percent loss of potential wealth** without ever losing your principal.

Here's a quick visual breakdown:

Scenario	Ending Balance
No Interruptions	$5,368,709
With 2% Fee	$2,988,313
With Two Withdrawls	$2,088,709
With Losses Only	$671,089
With 15% Tax	$559,732
With Losses + Tax + Fees	$51,368

Let that sink in for a minute. This is why what you don't see in your financial strategy hurts you the most. Imagine if you didn't have to worry about that 2 percent fee quietly eating away at your returns, or losing momentum every time you withdrew money, or stressing over taxes and market losses. What if there was a vehicle that allowed your money to keep growing—uninterrupted, predictable, and protected—no matter what was happening in the economy? If something like that existed, wouldn't it be worth learning everything you could about it?

You Finance Everything You Buy

One of my mentors, the late great R. Nelson Nash, wrote about a simple yet mind-blowing concept in his famous book, *Becoming Your Own Banker*. Now this may seem obvious to you at first, but when I truly read and understood it, it was groundbreaking for me.

Nelson wrote: "You finance everything you buy. You either pay interest to someone else, or you give up the interest you could have earned yourself."

That single realization completely reframed how I viewed money and debt. It allowed me to recognize that every financial decision has an opportunity cost—whether we borrow, pay cash, or invest, we're always moving dollars that could have been working for us. Understanding that principle is what ultimately led me to start digging more into the idea of strategic compounding, and how myself and others could utilize a properly structured whole life policy as the base foundation allowing us to create a banking style system we had complete control over.

The solution isn't just "earn more" or "spend less." The solution is to keep as much of your money as possible compounding while still having access to it when you need it.

The Three Money Archetypes

To make this crystal clear, let me show you three different ways people handle money. Most people bounce between the first two their entire lives, never realizing there's a third option.

Archetype 1: The Debtor

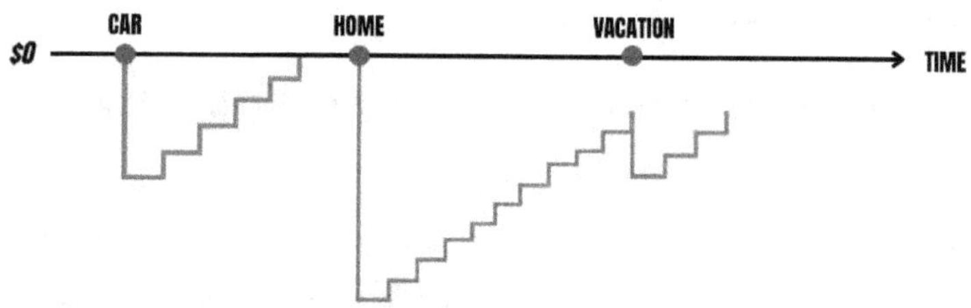

- Always spends more than they earn.
- Borrows money to solve problems.
- Makes payments, then repeats the cycle.
- Pays endless interest, never gets ahead.

They go into debt to make purchases, then work themselves back to the zero line. This is where the majority of Americans live, trapped in a loop of dependency and stress.

Archetype 2: The Saver

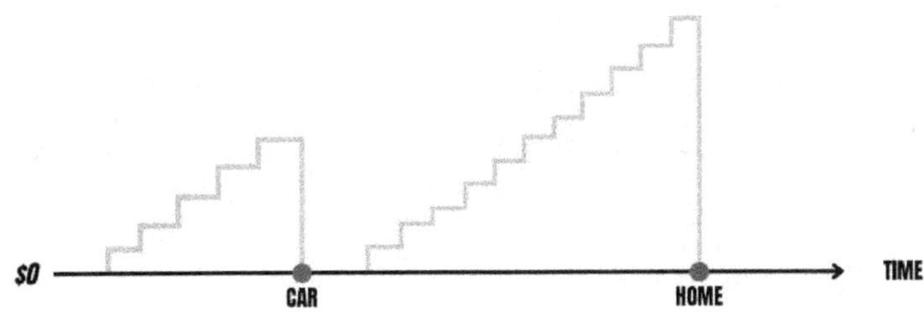

- More disciplined than the Debtor.

- Saves up before spending.

- Avoids interest payments, but forfeits growth potential.

- Interrupts compounding every time they use cash.

Savers feel more secure than Debtors, and they should; they're definitely better off. But they're still losing. Their money is never truly working for them long term because they keep pulling it out to use it.

Archetype 3: The Strategic Compounding Creator

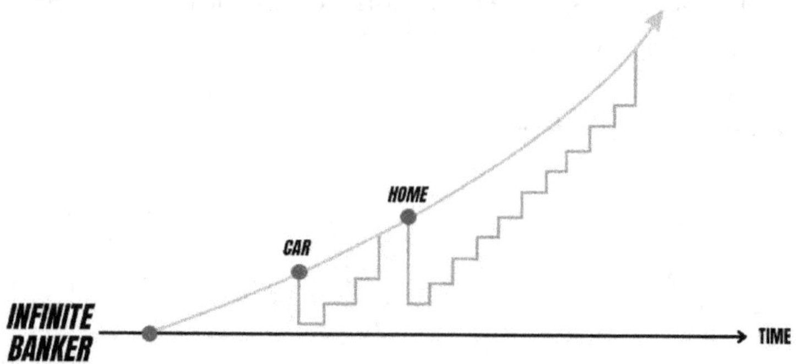

- Saves consistently.

- Uses savings as collateral instead of draining them.

- Borrows against their assets while their money keeps compounding.

- Repays loans on their own timeline with interest that shrinks over time.

This is the category you want to live in, and it's exactly what we're going to teach you how to do.

Here's how it works: Instead of spending your cash directly, you use it as collateral for loans. That means your money never leaves your system—it stays safely inside your family banking policy, continuing to earn uninterrupted compound growth year after year. At the same time, you gain access to capital through a policy loan, which is simply using the insurance company's money, secured by your own cash value.

This approach allows you to make purchases, pay off debt, or invest—*without ever interrupting the compounding process on your own dollars.* It's like having your cake and eating it too: Your money keeps working for you in one place while you simultaneously put it to work somewhere else. You're essentially creating velocity and efficiency within your own economy—your dollars don't just have one job anymore; they now perform multiple functions at once, building wealth faster and with more control.

I'll touch on this concept in much greater detail in a later chapter.

Here's the fundamental shift that separates wealth builders from everyone else: **They don't think about spending money. They think about deploying capital.**

When you spend money, it's gone. When you deploy capital, it goes to work and potentially comes back with friends.

From Compound Control to Capital Leverage

You now understand how crucial it is to protect your compounding engine, and how small interruptions can cost you millions over time, but here's where things get really exciting:

What if you could grow your wealth using money that wasn't even yours?

This is exactly what banks have been doing for centuries. They don't grow by saving more money; they grow by leveraging Other People's Money (OPM) while still earning uninterrupted returns on their own reserves (FYI, they use our money).

Think about it: When you deposit $10,000 in a bank account, they don't keep that money sitting in a vault. They immediately lend most of it out to someone else at a higher interest rate than they pay you. Your money works for them while their money works for them too.

Now that you've recovered and redirected your cash, it's not only time to start thinking like a bank; it's time to build yourself a system that allows you to operate like a bank too.

In the next chapter, we'll explore exactly how banks make money and why understanding their model is crucial to building your own wealth. You'll learn the five principles that every successful bank follows, and how you can apply those same principles to your personal finances. Then, we'll show you how to build your own "Warehouse of Wealth," a system that grows your money while keeping it accessible, gives you the borrowing power of a bank, and puts you in control of your financial future.

FAMILY BANKING

CHAPTER 7

The Private Banking Strategy

If I asked you to name the most profitable business in the world, what would you say? Tech companies? Oil giants? Big pharma?

Most people don't realize that one of the most consistently profitable models isn't in Silicon Valley or some Wall Street skyscraper. It's sitting right in your hometown.

Banks are everywhere, from small towns to major cities. They occupy those marble-floored buildings with massive advertising budgets. But here's the truth: Banks don't build wealth by owning money; they build wealth by controlling money. Your money, to be specific.

Let me break that down for you. When you deposit money into your bank account, it probably feels like you're doing something responsible, and to some degree, you are. What you may not realize is that in the eyes of the bank, your deposit is now a liability. It's money they owe back to you, plus a tiny sliver of interest.

So the moment your money hits their account, the bank flips it. They lend it out to someone else at a much higher rate than they pay you.

- You might earn 0.05 percent on your savings.

- Meanwhile, they loan it out as a personal loan at 9 percent, a car loan at 6 percent, or a credit card at 20-plus percent.

Here's a simple example: You deposit $10,000. The bank pays you a generous 1 percent interest, meaning you earn $100 for the year. The bank then loans that same $10,000 to a small business at 6 percent. That $10,000, your $10,000, now earns the bank $600. Subtract the $100 they pay you, and they net $500 for doing nothing but controlling the flow of money.

That's a 500 percent return on the spread, and they didn't put up a single dollar of their own capital.

The Numbers Don't Lie: Banking is a Goldmine

Here are some eye-opening statistics about how profitable banking really is:

- **Chase Bank** reported a record net income of $58.5 billion in 2024. That's $160 million per day.[7]

---

7   *JPMorgan Chase Reports Record Full-Year 2024 Net Income of $58.5 Billion."* JPMorgan Chase Press Release, January 12, 2025. https://www.jpmorganchase.com/news-stories

- **Chase Bank's Revenue** reached $177.6 billion in 2024, up 12.3 percent from the previous year.[8]

- The average checking account earns **0.07 percent** while the average personal loan charges **11.48 percent**. That's a 164x difference.[9]

- According to the FDIC, U.S. banks held $17.88 trillion in deposits in 2024, while earning 268.2 billion in profits. This represented a 5.6 percent increase from the previous year. (fdic.gov).[10]

Thanks to our good friend, fractional reserve banking, banks can loan out portions of those same dollars to multiple clients at once, collecting spreads on each transaction, while only being obligated to pay you your measly $100 in interest.

Banks don't build their empires by owning massive amounts of capital. They build them by becoming the gatekeepers of money and charging rent on every dollar that flows through their system.

"You are not the bank's customer. You are the bank's product." – Caleb Guilliams, *The AND Asset*

Private Banking

To become your own banker, you need to understand and apply the same principles that make banks highly efficient. Here are the five key principles banks master, and how you can use them to build your own system:

---

8   *Annual Report 2024: Financial Results.*" JPMorgan Chase Investor Relations, 2025. https://www.jpmorganchase.com/ir/annual-report

9   *Quarterly Banking Profile, Fourth Quarter 2024.*" FDIC, February 2025. https:// www.fdic.gov/analysis/quarterly-banking-profile

10   *National Rates and Rate Caps – Weekly Update: Average Interest Rate on Savings Accounts and Personal Loans.*" Data retrieved January 2025. https://fred.stlouisfed.org

1. Flow

Banks are absolute masters at directing the flow of money.

- Direct deposit ensures your paycheck flows through them first.

- Wall Street engineered 401(k)s so money flows directly into investments before you ever get to touch it.

- The IRS mandates tax withholdings before you get a dime.

Banks, Wall Street, and the IRS don't need to own your money. They just need to control it before you do. Imagine being able to make money on all the tax money you paid before the government got their cut.

Your goal: Build a system where you control the flow of your money. The sooner your money flows to you, the sooner you can put it to work. In the upcoming chapters, I'll break down how setting up a properly structured whole life policy built for family banking will allow you to apply all five of these principles at once.

2. Leverage

Leverage means multiplying your money's impact without multiplying your risk.

Example: You deposit $1,000. The bank pays you 1 percent interest, so their liability is $1,010. They loan it at 4 percent, bringing in $1,040. After repaying you, they pocket $30. That's a 300 percent return on the spread, they spent $10 (their control cost) to earn $40. That's banking at its finest.

Real Bank Leverage Statistics:

- Wells Fargo's net interest margin in 2024: **2.73 percent** (down from 3.06 percent in 2023 because of the rate environment).

- Citigroup's return on assets in Q2 2025: **0.59 percent** (meaning they earn 59 cents for every $100 in assets).

- The average community bank operates with a **10:1 leverage ratio** (for every $1 in capital, they control $10 in assets).

The power isn't in the amount; it's in the system. Small profits, multiplied across huge volumes, create massive wealth.

Because banks control the flow of money, they get tens of thousands of opportunities like this every single day.

Your goal: Leverage your capital more efficiently. Learn how to use Other People's Money safely and strategically to increase your returns without taking unnecessary risks.

3. Liquidity

Liquidity means having access to cash when you need it, without penalties, restrictions, or waiting periods. Banks prioritize liquidity because they never know when they'll need to meet withdrawal demands or capitalize on opportunities. You should do the same.

Most people trap their money in retirement accounts, home equity, or long-term investments they can't touch without getting hammered by penalties. True financial freedom comes from being able to move when opportunities (or emergencies) arise.

Your private banking strategy ensures that a portion of your capital is always safe, available, and growing in an environment you can access anytime, no matter what.

Your goal: Maintain access to cash, not just for protection, but for control.

4. Collateral

Banks don't take unnecessary risks; they collateralize everything. Every loan is backed by something the bank can claim if the deal goes sideways.

- Mortgages = backed by homes.

- Auto loans = backed by cars.

- Margin loans = backed by stocks.

Collateral reduces their risk and secures predictable returns. This explains why collateralized loans have lower interest rates than uncollateralized loans like credit cards. There's less risk for the lender.

Your goal: Use collateral to your advantage. Assets like the cash value in a properly structured whole life insurance policy can serve as powerful collateral, letting you borrow at low rates while your money continues to grow. You're not sacrificing your asset; you're leveraging it safely.

5. Velocity

Velocity is how fast money moves through your system. The faster the turnover, the harder each dollar works.

Banks never let money sit idle. Deposits are flipped into loans, repaid, and re-lent over and over. One dollar generates multiple income streams through high velocity. The bank's goal is to squeeze as many uses out of each dollar as possible.

You can't replicate their scale, but you can absolutely adopt their mindset. Using tools like your private family banking system (which we'll dive into in the next chapter), you can have money growing in one place while accessing it for other uses like investments, business opportunities, real estate—the possibilities are endless. That's how you multiply the velocity of your dollars.

Your goal: Create velocity in your own financial system. Use tools that let you multiply the uses of your money without giving up control.

Real-World Example: The Johnson Family Private Banking System

Let me show you how this actually works in practice. I connected with a family not too long ago—we'll call them the Johnson family. They were a couple in their early forties who were tired of traditional banking controlling their financial future.

Their Starting Point:

- Combined income: $120,000/year

- Savings account: $45,000 earning 0.05 percent

- 401(k) balances: $85,000

- Monthly cash flow available: $2,500

The Problem: Their money was scattered across different accounts, earning almost nothing, and they had minimal access to capital for opportunities without penalties, loan applications, or interrupting their current growth.

The Solution: I helped them implement a private banking strategy using a properly structured whole life insurance policy, combined with a systematic approach to income stacking.

What They Did:

Year 1 to 2: Foundation Building

- They redirected $30,000 of their savings into a specially designed whole life policy[11] as initial funding.

- They began contributing $2,000/month into the policy (reducing 401(k) contributions).

- After eighteen months, they used a $25,000 policy loan[12] (a tax-free loan from the insurance company using their cash value as collateral) to pay off high-interest credit cards, then took the monthly payments that were previously being paid to those credit cards and paid the loan back they took from their own policy, aka their family banking system.

Year 3: First Income Stream

- They took another $35,000 policy loan, but this time it was for a real estate down payment.

---

11   A customized form of whole life insurance structured for maximum cash value growth and minimum death benefit costs. It uses a blend of base premium and paid-up additions (PUAs) to create early liquidity and maximize long-term internal rate of return — often used as the foundation for Infinite Banking.

12   A tax-free loan you have access to from the insurance company's general pool of funds using your cash value as collateral. You're not withdrawing your money; you're leveraging it. Your cash value continues to grow as if you never touched it, while you control repayment terms — just like a banker would.

- That 35K helped them purchase a rental property generating $350/month net income.

- They began using rental income to pay back their policy loan, giving themselves the ability to borrow the cash out again when the next opportunity presented itself.

Year 4 to 5: Income Stacking in Action

- They started a second policy with $500/month from rental income plus a bit of extra cash flow.

- They used a $20,000 loan from their original policy to invest in private lending at 12 percent returns. (I'll touch more on private lending and what that process looks like in Chapter 10.)

- Their 12 percent private lending generated them $200/month in additional income.

- At this point, they had built $550/month in passive income and added one rental property to their growing portfolio.

- Their first policy is now at the point we call the "efficiency zone," meaning when they put money in, more money than they put in shows up as usable cash.

Year 6: The Velocity Effect

- After six years of paying their policy premium and funneling their passive cash flow back into their family banking system, they took an additional $40,000 policy loan.

- This time, they invested it in a second rental property.

- Their total passive income grew to $900/month.

- Some of that passive income now funds a third policy at $600/month.

The Income Stacking Insight: Every eighteen to twenty-four months, the Johnsons systematically used their growing passive income to either fund new policies or take additional loans to disburse into income-producing investments. Each new income stream accelerated the next cycle, creating what's known as the "velocity of money" effect. Their money wasn't just working in one place; it was working in multiple places simultaneously while continuing to compound in their policies.

The Key Transformation: Instead of remaining customers who paid interest to traditional banks, the Johnsons decided to become their own bankers. They took a closer look at where their money was flowing and realized that much of it was sitting idle or leaving their household economy altogether. By redirecting lazy cash from their savings account, reallocating funds they no longer wanted locked away in their 401(k), and capturing dollars that were previously flowing out to third-party debts, they built a guaranteed, ever-increasing pool of capital they could leverage to start creating usable wealth immediately.

They discovered that their savings account wasn't truly helping them—it was safe, but stagnant. Their 401(k) had growth potential but no control or access. And their high-interest debts were simply accelerating the transfer of their most valuable dollars to someone else's system. By adding just one strategic step into their financial equation—running their money through their own family banking system first—they completely changed their financial trajectory.

Now, every dollar the Johnsons earn passes through their control, compounds continuously, and can be leveraged to stack investments that pay passive income they can actually use today—all while protecting their family with an ever-increasing death benefit that strengthens their legacy.

How Does This Work?

The principles are clear. The mindset shift is real. But you might be wondering: *This sounds great in theory, but how does it actually work?*

That's exactly what we're covering in the next chapter. We'll dive into the Strategic Compounding Mindset and show you how to align your money so it grows year after year, uninterrupted, and under your complete control.

You'll learn about the most flexible financial asset available on the market. One that lets you store your cash, keep it compounding, and borrow against it to fund all of life's opportunities, without disrupting the growth.

But before we got into the specific vehicle, you needed to understand the philosophy behind it. Banks have been using these five principles for centuries to build massive wealth. Now it's your turn to use them for your family's benefit.

Banks are incredibly successful at building and maintaining wealth. Instead of resenting that success, we're going to study it, understand it, and apply those same principles to your personal finances. Because, at the end of the day, if you're not thinking like a bank, you're probably getting taken advantage of by one.

It's time to flip the script.

CHAPTER 8

Building Your Warehouse of Wealth

Note: The information in this chapter is for educational purposes. Policy performance will vary based on company, structure, and use. Work with a qualified infinite banking practitioner to design a system appropriate for your specific situation.

Before you can build your Warehouse of Wealth, you need to understand the different tools available—and why most of them simply weren't designed for what we're trying to accomplish. Let's take a closer look at the most common types of life insurance and how they function.

Term Life Insurance

Term life is the simplest and cheapest form of coverage. You pay a fixed premium for a set period—typically ten, twenty, or thirty years—and if you pass away during that term, your beneficiaries receive the death benefit. Statistically, that happens less than 2 percent of the time, which is why term insurance can be priced so cheap.

While a term policy is great for *temporary* protection needs, it does absolutely nothing for *wealth building*. When the term ends, the policy expires, and if you're still alive, all the money you paid in premiums is gone. There's no cash value, no compounding, and no financial leverage. It's pure protection—not a financial strategy.

Index Universal Life Insurance (IUL)

Indexed Universal Life is often sold as a modern upgrade to Whole Life. An IUL can be explained as a life insurance policy with market-linked growth. Instead of a guaranteed rate, your cash value growth is tied to an index like the S&P 500. When the market rises, you earn interest up to a cap rate; when it falls, you often earn 0 percent thanks to a floor.

Sounds great in theory—until you realize your money isn't actually in the market. The insurance company controls the rules: They set the caps, participation rates, and internal costs. As those change, your returns drop. Over time, rising expenses and lowered caps can drain performance, leaving policyholders disappointed.

Whole Life, by contrast, isn't built on assumptions. It offers guaranteed growth, steady dividends, and predictable access to capital—the essential ingredients for infinite banking. If your goal is to build long-term, stable wealth you can actually control, properly structured Whole Life remains the gold standard.

Variable Universal Life Insurance (VUL)

Variable Life takes things a step further by tying your policy's cash value directly to market investments—mutual funds or subaccounts you choose. This means your policy's performance fluctuates with the market. While that might sound appealing in a bull market, it exposes your cash value to potential losses, higher fees, and complex management.

The issue is control. You're no longer guaranteed compounding; you're simply speculating. And when your goal is to build a personal banking system that depends on steady, uninterrupted growth, volatility is the last thing you want.

Whole Life Insurance (WL)

Whole Life is the original and most stable form of permanent insurance. It provides a guaranteed death benefit, level premiums, and a cash value that grows predictably every year. The cash value earns a guaranteed interest rate and—if issued by a mutual insurance company—can also receive annual dividends based on the company's profits.

This combination of guaranteed growth, tax advantages, and liquidity through policy loans is what makes properly structured whole life the ideal foundation for building a family banking system. It gives you a place to store and access capital—safely, privately, and predictably—while maintaining long-term protection for your family.

Why Dividend-Paying Whole Life from a Mutual Company is the Only Fit for Infinite Banking

Infinite banking isn't about chasing returns—it's about **regaining control of your capital**. Only a *dividend-paying* whole life policy from a *mutual company* provides:

- **Guaranteed growth** - steady, compounding increases every single year.

- **Uninterrupted compounding** - even when you borrow against your cash value.

- **Liquidity and control** - access to funds without penalties, taxes, or restrictions.

- **Privacy and protection** - your policy is a private contract, not a government-registered account.

- **Legacy benefits** - an ever-increasing death benefit that strengthens your family's financial foundation.

That's why infinite banking practitioners don't use term, universal, or variable life—those tools weren't designed for this purpose. We're not looking for speculation or temporary coverage. We're building a **permanent, predictable, and privately controlled banking system** that allows your dollars to work harder, longer, and smarter—just like the banks do.

Now that you understand why we use this specific product over others, I want to take a moment to address the elephant in the room. You've probably been told your entire life that whole life insurance is a "bad investment." Hell, Suze Orman and Dave Ramsey have both built their careers on telling people to "buy term and invest the difference."

Here's the thing: They're not wrong about traditional whole life insurance. Most policies sold by insurance agents are structured to maximize death benefit, not available cash value. They're designed for insurance purposes, not banking purposes. When properly structured for infinite banking, whole life insurance becomes something entirely different, a powerful financial tool that gives you the control and flexibility banks have been using for centuries.

Why Most People Store Money in the Wrong Warehouse

Ask the average American where they keep their wealth and you'll hear:

- My 401(k)

- My savings account

- My house

- My Roth IRA

- Sometimes even crypto or ETFs

Here's the issue: Each of those "warehouses" comes with restrictions. Either limited access, market volatility, delayed growth, tax penalties, or all of the above. Worse, none of them offer uninterrupted compounding and complete control at the same time.

When you place your money into those traditional accounts, you're essentially handing it over to someone else's warehouse like the government's, the bank's, or Wall Street's. That means you're no longer in control.

Your Warehouse of Wealth flips that equation. This isn't about replacing every financial tool you have; if you love the market you can still invest in it. This is about creating a base layer that works

24/7, a pool of capital that compounds quietly in the background and stays accessible whenever you need it.

The Numbers Behind Whole Life Insurance Success

Let me share some statistics that might surprise you about who actually uses whole life insurance:

- **Bank-Owned Life Insurance (BOLI):** U.S. banks held over $190 billion in life insurance policies in 2023, with the top ten banks holding an average of $7.8 billion each.

- **Corporate-Owned Life Insurance (COLI):** Fortune 500 companies hold over $4 trillion in corporate-owned life insurance policies, and it's not because it's the cool thing to do. They understand the value of a guaranteed and flexible asset.

- **High Net Worth Usage:** "Research shows that as household financial wealth increases, the likelihood of owning life insurance rises by roughly 11–13 percentage points for every additional $100,000 of wealth."[13]

These aren't financial novices making emotional decisions. These are institutions and individuals who have access to every investment vehicle available, yet they choose whole life insurance for a significant portion of their assets. Why? Because they understand something most people don't: It's not about the rate of return; it's about the rate of control.

---

13   Gropper, M., & Kuhnen, C. M. (2023). *Wealth and Insurance Choices: Evidence from U.S. Households.*

What Makes a Policy Work for Infinite Banking

Infinite Banking Concept (IBC): The process of becoming your own banker by utilizing a specially designed, dividend-paying whole life insurance policy to finance the needs of your daily life—allowing you to recapture the interest you would have otherwise lost to third-party institutions. Instead of letting banks, lenders, or credit cards profit from your cash flow, infinite banking gives you the ability to keep that money circulating within your own system, compounding and working for your benefit.

Here's the truth: Not all life insurance policies are created equal.

You can't just call up Jake from State Farm and say, "Give me a whole life policy," and expect it to work like a private bank. If it's not structured correctly, your policy will:

- Grow too slowly, limiting your long-term potential.

- Provide little to no liquidity in the early years.

- Fail to function as your personal banking system, preventing you from truly controlling and leveraging your capital.

Most policies on the market are designed to maximize death benefit, not cash value. The death benefit is extremely important, don't get me wrong. I believe protecting your family should be your number one priority, but we can solve for that large number another way. The death benefit is not the main focus when building a policy for infinite banking.

What Qualifies a Policy for Infinite Banking:

Before I explain what the qualifications are for a policy to be used for infinite banking I want to cover some quick definitions in case this is your first time ever being exposed to this concept or whole life insurance in general.

Specially Designed Whole Life (SDWL)

A customized form of whole life insurance structured for maximum cash value growth and minimum death benefit costs. It uses a blend of base premium and paid-up additions (PUAs) to create early liquidity and maximize long-term internal rate of return—often used as the foundation for infinite banking.

Death Benefit

The total tax-free amount paid to beneficiaries when the insured person passes away. In an IBC design, the death benefit also acts as a financial safety net and guarantees legacy transfer.

Cash Value

The savings or equity portion of a whole life policy that grows over time. It earns guaranteed interest and non-guaranteed dividends (from participating mutual companies). The cash value is accessible to the policy owner via withdrawals or policy loans while continuing to compound uninterrupted.

Paid-Up Additions (PUAs)

Additional mini "paid-in-full" insurance policies that boost both cash value and death benefit immediately. PUAs are the main engine of growth early on in a properly structured policy and are often funded with flexible overpayments beyond the base premium.

Base Premium

The core cost of maintaining the whole life policy. It funds the guaranteed portion of the death benefit and establishes the policy's foundation. A well-structured policy typically keeps the base premium between 25 to 50 percent of the total payment to maximize flexibility and cash value.

Policy Loan

A tax-free loan you have access to from the insurance company's general pool of funds using your cash value as collateral. You're not withdrawing your money; you're leveraging it. Your cash value continues to grow as if you never touched it, while you control repayment terms—just like a banker would.

Loan Interest

The interest charged by the insurance company when you borrow against your cash value. This interest goes back to the company's general fund, which contributes to future dividends shared among policyholders. Generally between 4 to 6 percent simple interest.

Guaranteed Growth Rate

The minimum annual rate of return credited to your cash value, regardless of outside market influences. Typically ranges between 2.5 to 4 percent (depending on the company), providing stability and predictability over time.

Dividends

A share of the insurance company's profits distributed to policyholders of participating (mutual) companies. Dividends are not guaranteed but have been paid consistently for well over 100-plus years by the strongest insurance companies. They can be used in multiple different ways. Some of the most popular are to purchase more PUAs (Paid-Up Additions), reduce premiums, or simply received as a check.

Mutual Insurance Company

A policyholder-owned company, meaning there are no outside shareholders—the profits go back to participating policyholders in the form of dividends. This ownership structure aligns perfectly with the infinite banking philosophy of keeping control within your system.

Modified Endowment Contract (MEC)

A policy classification by the IRS that occurs when too much premium is paid relative to the death benefit, causing your policy to lose certain tax advantages like tax-free growth and access without penalty before age fifty-nine and a half. MEC policies grow tax-deferred, like a 401(k) or IRA, and withdrawals and loans become taxable. Properly structured policies are designed to avoid MEC status throughout the life of the policy.

Surrender Value

The amount available if you cancel (surrender) your policy, representing the accumulated cash value minus any surrender charges or outstanding loans.

Overfunding

The act of intentionally paying more premium into your policy (via PUAs) to accelerate cash value growth and enhance long-term efficiency—without triggering a MEC.

Uninterrupted Compounding

The principle that your dollars continue earning compound interest even when borrowed against, since loans are collateralized, not withdrawals. This is the cornerstone of the infinite banking strategy.

Now that I've covered some of the common terms used when discussing dividend paying whole life insurance and infinite banking, I'll explain what qualifies a policy for the use of infinite banking.

1. It's Whole Life, Not Universal Life

Whole life insurance provides guaranteed growth, predictable performance, and contractual certainty—the kind of stability you can build a system on.

Universal life, on the other hand—whether it's indexed or variable—comes with moving parts, market risk, and rising internal costs over time.

If your goal is to build a banking system that lasts, you need reliability, not guesswork. Consistency is what keeps your financial foundation strong decade after decade.

2. It's From a Mutual Company

Mutual life insurance companies are owned by their policyholders, not Wall Street shareholders. That means the company's first priority is serving you, not chasing quarterly stock earnings.

When the company performs well, it shares a portion of the surplus with policyholders in the form of dividends (not guaranteed, but many companies have paid them for well over 100 years straight with some of the oldest topping out at 160-plus years). You can use those dividends to buy more paid-up insurance, which quietly boosts your overall death benefit, cash value and future dividend over time.

Working with a mutual company is important because your interests and the company's interests are aligned. The value you help create by taking and repaying loans with interest flows back to you and other policyholders over time.

3. It's Structured for High Early Cash Value

Think of your policy as a rocketship made up of two parts:

- The body of the rocket is represented by the base of your policy. This portion of the policy is extremely important because it heavily affects your policies long-term cash growth potential and is responsible for 90-plus percent of your policies death benefit. This portion of the policy's overall premium will be required to be paid for the life of the policy.

- The second part of the rocket ship is the booster rockets. Think of these as your Paid-Up Additions (PUAs)—the boosters that give your policy an extra surge of power in the early years. They accelerate both cash value growth and liquidity, helping your system take off faster. In the beginning, you want to funnel as much fuel (your money) into these boosters as possible, because their job is to launch your policy into orbit. Once they've done that— once your policy is self-sustaining—they naturally fall away, leaving the main engine (your base policy) to carry the mission forward.

We tune the mix so more money flows into your booster rockets early on, without going so extreme that it hurts long-term performance or risks MEC issues. Remember: MEC means you've put more cash into your policy than it can legally hold so it becomes a taxable asset. This is going to be different for every individual situation.

When done correctly your policy will have usable cash value fast, often available to borrow against within the first thirty days, all while still keeping a strong foundation for future growth.

4. It Avoids MEC Status

Think of a MEC (Modified Endowment Contract) limit like a "fill line" on your policy. If you pour in too much premium too fast, which is determined by your specific policy design, the IRS changes the rules:

- Don't worry, the death benefit is still protected and paid out tax-free, but…

- Loans and withdrawals become taxable, plus there are penalties for accessing the cash if you're under fifty-nine and a half years old.

Once a policy becomes a MEC, it can't be undone. It's important to note that any well-run insurance company will alert you multiple times that your policy is in danger of crossing that MEC line if you try to stuff it with more cash than it can hold at any one point. A good coach will not only design funding to stay safely under the line, with room for flexibility, but they'll educate you on how to make sure your policy never crosses that MEC line. Later in the book, I'll tell you exactly where you can find a list of certified infinite banking coaches like myself to learn from.

5. It's Built With Long-Term Funding in Mind

The real power comes from consistent contributions over time. Whether you fund monthly or annually, think of this as your family's opportunity warehouse. The steadier you stock it, the more financial muscle it builds.

Our designs set a sustainable baseline you can maintain for years, with room to add extra deposits when you have a surplus, all so you can grow cash value, strengthen the death benefit, and expand your borrowing capacity without risking MEC issues.

Real-Life Numbers: What Early Growth Looks Like

Let me show you what properly structured policy growth actually looks like. This example assumes a thirty-five-year-old female funding a policy with $30,000 per year which is represented under (Premium Paid):

Year	Age	Premium Paid	Net Cash Value	Net Death Benefit
1	36	$30,000	$20,552	$918,617
2	37	$60,000	$42,190	$1,009,883
3	38	$90,000	$68,585	$1,100,684
4	39	$120,000	$99,567	$1,190,603
5	40	$150,000	$131,858	$1,279,665
10	45	$300,000	$316,267	$1,712,822
15	50	$450,000	$546,714	$2,136,034
20	55	$600,000	$831,460	$2,554,764

These numbers are based on current dividend scales and are not guaranteed.

Column one represents the **Policy Year**, while column two shows the age you'll be turning during that year. The Premium Paid column reflects the total amount of premium contributed to the policy up to that point. Column four, **Net Cash Value**, shows the liquid portion of the policy—the amount available to you through a policy loan. The final column, **Net Death Benefit**, represents the total tax-free payout your beneficiaries would receive if the insured (in this case, the thirty-five-year-old) were to pass away during that policy year.

Remember, the core purpose of insurance is to transfer risk. In this example, the thirty-five-year-old female is transferring that risk to the insurance company by committing $30,000 per year into a whole life policy. In return, the company guarantees her a tax-free death benefit starting at $918,617—effectively transforming a smaller sum of money into a much larger, guaranteed asset that protects her family and builds lasting wealth. In this specific scenario, only the base premium of $9,000 is required on an annual basis. The additional $21,000 is the flexible Paid-Up Additions or (extra cash) she's funneling into the policy.

Notice a few key things:

- By year four, the annual cash value growth is greater than her $30,000 yearly premium (Year four cash value $99,567 minus year three cash value $68,585 = $30,982).

- By year ten, she has more cash value than she's contributed ($316,672 vs. $300,000).

- By year fifteen, the system is generating significant wealth above her contributions.

- Throughout her entire life, the death benefit and cash values continue to grow automatically through annual premium payments and/or earned dividends.

I want to make this very clear. The girl in this example is not practicing infinite banking. All she is currently doing is heavily funding her policy with additional cash. If she were to start utilizing her policy to practice infinite banking (taking loans and repaying them with market rate interest) over the twenty-year period, both her cash value and her death benefit would grow significantly larger than what's represented in the illustration above.

If $30,000 a year sounds like a lot—believe me, I get it. The exact same process can be started with as little as $5,000 or $10,000 per year. The key difference is that, unlike locking your money away in a qualified plan such as a 401(k), a large portion of these dollars remains accessible for whatever opportunities or needs arise. Don't think about it as a payment; think about it as your new banking system that provides you with countless benefits.

Where you start doesn't matter—the banking function and compounding growth work the same on a $5,000 policy as they do on a $50,000 policy. What matters most is that you start the compounding clock and put your dollars to work inside a system you control as soon as possible.

Using Policy Loans: Access Without Interruption

Here's where the system gets powerful. When you need access to cash, you don't withdraw funds from your policy. Instead, you take a collateralized loan from the insurance company using your cash value to back it.

That means:

- Your money stays in the policy.

- It continues to grow and earn dividends.

- You can use the loan for anything: investing, paying off debt, buying equipment, funding opportunities, etc.

- You set the repayment terms.

Current loan rates are typically around 4 to 6 percent simple interest (varies by company). But here's the beautiful part: You get to decide when to make payments, how much to pay, or whether to pay anything back at all during your lifetime.

Why? Because you're in control. You're the banker. Now you might be wondering how in the world does that work? Remember: When you take a loan from your policy, all you're doing is leveraging the access you have to a portion of your current death benefit. That means if you pass away with an outstanding loan balance, the loan amount gets subtracted from your death benefit and the remaining portion will be paid out to your family tax-free.

This is where building passive cash flow integrates perfectly with traditional infinite banking. Instead of just using your policy as a savings vehicle, you can systematically use policy loans to create multiple income streams that fund additional policies and investments.

Here's how it works:

1. **Foundation Phase:** Build up the cash value in your first policy.

2. **First Investment:** Use a policy loan to purchase an income-producing asset (rental property, private lending, etc.).

3. **Income Reinvestment:** Use passive income to fund additional policies or investments.

4. **Systematic Stacking:** Every three to eighteen months, deploy new capital into additional income streams depending on the type.

5. **Acceleration:** Each new income stream helps fund the next cycle faster.

This creates what's known as the velocity of money; your dollars work in multiple places simultaneously while continuing to compound in your policies.

A Note on Repayment Strategy

While you control 100 percent of your repayment plan, I recommend treating your policy loan like a real loan. Set up a schedule and make regular payments, even if small. Treat your money like you would the bank's, if not better.

Why? Because the money you repay goes back into your policy and becomes available again to borrow, creating a recycling effect. You're not just spending; you're recapturing. This is the essence of the strategic compounding we talked about earlier.

Plus, if you're using the income stacking approach I mentioned in Chapter 7 when referencing the Johnson family, your passive income can systematically pay down loans while funding new opportunities, creating a self-sustaining cycle.

Buying a Car Utilizing Infinite Banking

Let's take a look at what it actually means to *be your own banker* using a real-life example—buying a car.

Imagine in this example Mr. Smith decides to deposit $2,000 per month—that's $24,000 a year—into a properly structured, dividend-paying whole life policy as premium.

Year 1: His first deposit buys $596,305 in death benefit and creates $13,921 in cash value. That cash value is available immediately, but instead of accessing it, he decides to let it grow for now.

Year 2: Another $24,000 in premium goes into the policy. Again, his death benefit rises. This time to $638,877, and his available cash value nearly doubles to $28,386.

Year 3: After a third premium deposit, his death benefit climbs to $681,691 and his cash value hits $50,858. At this point, he decides it's time to buy that new car he's been eyeing.

Now, here's where things get interesting. Instead of walking into a bank or dealership and hoping he gets approved for the loan, he simply calls the insurance company and requests a $50,000 policy loan. Within a few days, that money is sitting in his checking account—no credit check, no underwriting, no stress.

Mr. Smith now owns the title to his $50,000 car because he leveraged the cash value inside his policy to take a loan and make the purchase outright. Remember, his original $50,000 is still sitting in the policy, continuing to earn uninterrupted compounding growth. Instead of sending payments to a third-party lender, he chose to take the banking function into his own hands. As an honest banker, Mr. Smith knows that the $50,000 he accessed was simply a loan secured by his cash value. Because he wants to maintain financial discipline, he decides to repay it just like a traditional car loan—about $10,200 a year, or roughly 7 percent interest, for six years.

The key difference? **Control**. Mr. Smith sets the repayment terms himself. He can pay on a fixed schedule or in flexible, irregular amounts—whatever fits his situation. Either way, instead of letting the interest he would have paid to the third-party bank escape his system, he's now paying it back to himself allowing him to recapture and reuse it to grow his family banking system.

POLICY YEAR	AGE	POLICY PREMIUM DEPOSIT	CAR LOAN PAYMENT	CAR PURCHASE	CASH VALUE AVAILABLE	DEATH BENEFIT
1	45	$24,000			$13,921	$596,305
2	46	$24,000			$28,386	$638,877
3	47	$24,000	$10,200	$50,000	$50,858	$681,691
4	48	$24,000	$10,200		$34,524	$724,235
5	49	$24,000	$10,200		$68,861	$766,538
6	50	$9,600	$10,200		$89,848	$770,968
7	51	$9,600	$10,200		$111,145	$775,866
8	52	$9,600	$10,200		$132,603	$781,257
Total Premium & Loan Repaid: $210,000				Cash Value Growth: $132,603		

By year four, he adds another $24,000 premium. His death benefit increases again to $724,235, and his available cash value is now $34,524—*even while repaying his car loan.*

By year six, he decides to scale back his premium to $9,600 a year—because life happens. Maybe there's a new baby, a big move, or another priority. The beauty of a properly structured policy is flexibility: He can reduce deposits and still experience growth.

After eight years, here's the result:

- Total premiums paid: ($24,000 x 5) + ($9,600x3) = $148,800

- Borrowed for the car: $50,000

- Repaid to his system: $10,200 x 6 = $61,200

- Total premiums & loans repaid: $148,800 + $61,200 = $210,000

- Total available cash value: $132,603 + Title to 50K car

At this point, he's bought his car, paid himself back with interest, and his policy continues to grow—uninterrupted.

Six years after buying and paying off his car utilizing his banking system, the family is ready to purchase another vehicle. This time for his wife. Luckily Mr. Smith has been capitalizing his policy these last eight years, so he's currently sitting on $132,603 in available cash value. Because he saw how great financing one car through his family banking system worked, he decided, why not do a second. Instead of heading down to the bank to see if they can get approved for the loan, he borrows **$55,000** from his own system again, and sets up the same repayment terms as the first car—7 percent interest, $11,250 a year for six years.

POLICY YEAR	AGE	POLICY PREMIUM DEPOSIT	CAR LOAN PAYMENT	CAR PURCHASE	CASH VALUE AVAILABLE	DEATH BENEFIT
8	52	$9,600	$10,200		$132,603	$781,257
9	53	$9,600	$11,250	$55,000	$100,364	$787,154
10	54	$9,600	$11,250		$123,372	$793,544
11	55	$9,600	$11,250		$146,647	$800,408
12	56	$9,600	$11,250		$170,130	$807,758
13	57	$9,600	$11,250		$194,113	$815,560
14	58	$9,600	$11,250		$218,329	$823,831
Total Premium & Loan Repaid: $125,100				Cash Value Growth: $85,726		

Here's how it plays out:

- Premiums paid during this phase: $9,600 x 6 = $57,600
- Borrowed: $55,000
- Repaid: $11,250 x 6 = $67,500
- Net injection: $57,600 + $67,500 - $55,000 = $70,100
- Final cash value: **$218,329**

When you add it up, Mr. Smith not only financed *two vehicles*—he's actually grown his family's bank by **$85,726**, all while driving both cars.

That's what happens when you stop sending interest payments out and start keeping them in your system. The cars depreciate, sure—but his wealth didn't. His money kept compounding the entire time.

That's the real power of infinite banking: It allows your dollars to work in two places at once—growing wealth and funding life, simultaneously.

How to Get a Policy Set Up

Here's what you need to know:

1. Research Multiple Insurance Companies

Find out what they offer and get the underwriting process started. Not all companies are created equal, and not all agents understand how to properly structure a policy equipped for infinite banking. That's why teaming up with a certified infinite banking practitioner will save you a ton of time across the board and make sure you get the exact policy you're looking for from the company that best suits your needs.

2. Work with a Credentialed IBC (Infinite Banking Concepts) Practitioner

Their primary role is to design a policy that fits your goals, cash flow, and timeline. If you work with someone who isn't an IBC practitioner, the risk of getting a poorly structured policy that doesn't meet your banking needs increases dramatically.

Working with a certified infinite banking practitioner is completely free; they're compensated by the insurance company, so no additional cost is required from you. You can find an active list of practitioners near you at infinitebanking.org/practitioner-finder. You'll find my profile listed in my current home state of Florida by typing in my name. Understand there are others out there who teach this concept on a high level that are not certified practitioners. Whoever you choose to work with, be sure to do your necessary due diligence to make sure they are a good fit for you. The goal is to build a life long relationship with your coach/mentor, so be sure to work with someone you like.

3. Understand the Underwriting Process

Life insurance underwriting typically involves:

- Medical exam (blood work, basic physical)

- Financial qualification (proving you can afford the premiums)

- Sometimes additional requirements may be necessary like an APS (Attending Physician Statement) on certain medical records

The process can take anywhere from two to eight weeks from application to policy delivery. If you have pre-existing health conditions or don't personally qualify, don't worry, you do have the ability to open and own multiple policies on a spouse or child's life, which means you can still practice infinite banking yourself.

This Isn't Just Theory; It's How I Built My System

My wife and I didn't start with tons of extra cash. After selling some land and implementing some strict savings habits, we eventually had enough money set aside to start aggressively paying down the $60,000 in debt we owed.

We could have sent that money straight to creditors. Instead, we started our first policy, borrowed against it to systematically pay off debt, and repaid ourselves on our schedule all while our cash sat in the policy continuing to grow uninterrupted.

Now that policies plus multiple others are the source of our:

- Emergency funds

- Investment capital

- Travel funds

- Long-term legacy planning

- Our son's future business funding

It's not a savings account. It's not an investment. It's a financial base camp. It's the foundation everything else is built on.

You might be asking yourself, *Is one policy enough to meet my family's banking needs, or should I have more than one?*

Think about it this way: The bank you use today doesn't have just one branch. If it did, it'd be nearly impossible to serve all its customers effectively. In the beginning, that bank probably *did* start with a single location—but as it grew, it needed to expand to handle more deposits, more loans, and more opportunity. Your banking system works the same way. At some point—usually sooner than you think if you started small—your first policy will reach capacity and won't be able to efficiently hold all your cash flow. That's a good problem to have, and that's when it's time to expand.

The beauty of infinite banking is that you can open new "branches"—policies on yourself, your spouse, your children, your parents, or even business partners. Each one adds strength and flexibility to your overall system. One policy is a great start. But a network of policies working together—that's when you've built a true family banking system.

From Foundation to Implementation

You now understand how to build your Warehouse of Wealth, but having the warehouse is just the beginning. In the next chapter, we'll address the objections and skepticism you've probably been feeling as you read this.

After that, we'll dive into the real fun: putting your warehouse to work using Other People's Money to create multiple income streams while your capital continues to grow uninterrupted.

The wealthy understand this instinctively: Never interrupt your compounding unless absolutely necessary, and when you need capital, find ways to access it without disturbing your wealth-building engines. Now you understand it too. And that understanding is about to change everything you thought you knew about building wealth.

CHAPTER 9

Addressing the Objections

Now that you understand how to build your Warehouse of Wealth, I'm guessing you've got some questions or some doubts. Hell, maybe you're sitting there thinking, *This sounds too good to be true*, or, *My financial advisor is going to think I'm an idiot for suggesting this.*

I get it. I felt the same way.

Here's what changed my mind: I stopped listening to what people said about whole life insurance and started looking at what wealthy families actually do with their money. What I discovered was that many of the same financial experts telling regular people to avoid whole life insurance were using it themselves. We discussed how the banks use it, how corporations use it, and don't forget about the ultra-wealthy families who have used it for over a century.

So why the disconnect? Why do they tell you one thing but do another? One word: control!

This chapter addresses the most common objections to whole life insurance head-on, because if you're going to build your own private banking system, you need to understand exactly what you're getting into, and what you're not.

Objection #1: "Whole Life Insurance is a Bad Investment."

The Truth: Whole life insurance isn't an investment. It's a financial **tool**.

Comparing whole life insurance to the stock market is like comparing a Swiss Army knife to a race car. They serve completely different purposes, and judging one by the standards of the other misses the point entirely.

What Whole Life Insurance Actually Does:

- Provides guaranteed death benefit protection for your family.

- Creates tax-advantaged cash accumulation that grows every year guaranteed.

- Offers liquidity through policy loans without penalties or restrictions.

- Generates potential dividends from mutual companies (many for 125-plus years straight).

- Serves as collateral for other investments and opportunities.

- Protects against market volatility and economic uncertainty.

- Protects your wealth against lawsuits, judgements, and leans (in most states).

What the Stock Market Does:

- Provides potential for higher returns (with major emphasis on "potential").

- Comes with significant volatility and risk.

- Offers no guarantees whatsoever.

- Can lose substantial value during downturns (and will, repeatedly).

- Provides no death benefit protection.

- Tax treatment depends on account type and timing.

- Offers no protection from litigation.

Instead of comparing whole life to stocks, compare it to what it actually replaces in your financial plan:

Consideration	Whole Life	Savings Account	Stocks
100% Principal Protection	YES	YES	NO
Guaranteed Growth 3-5%	YES	NO	NO
Tax Deffered Growth	YES	NO	Until Sold
Protection From Creditors	YES	NO	NO
Disability Benefits	YES	NO	NO
Uninterrupted Compounding	YES	NO	NO
Tax Free Dividends	YES	NO	NO
No Market Volitity	YES	YES	NO
Death Benefit for Heirs	YES	NO	NO

When you compare apples to apples, whole life insurance suddenly looks significantly more attractive.

Objection #2: "The Fees and Surrender Charges Are Too High."

The Truth: This objection is based on misunderstanding how cash value builds and how the product works long term.

The Early Years: Yes, in the first few years, a portion of your premium goes toward:

- The death benefit cost (you're buying life insurance, after all).

- Company expenses.

- Agent compensation.

This is why we structure policies with Paid-Up Additions (PUAs) to accelerate cash value growth and minimize this early "capital crunch." We're not hiding this; we're designing around it. Remember earlier in the book when we discussed what types of management fees come with market investments? No single product is perfect.

The Long-Term Picture: Often between years four to six the premium you pay is surpassed by the cash value growth within the policy. By year ten to twelve you have access to every dollar you've put into the policy thus far—meaning the policy becomes self-sustaining. These timelines are averages and can be expedited by multiple years simply by continuing to max fund your policies Paid-Up Additions.

Surrender Charges vs. Opportunity Cost: The financial industry loves to criticize surrender charges while completely ignoring opportunity costs. Let's be honest about costs:

- Your savings account has no surrender charges, but you're losing 3 to 6 percent annually to inflation.

- Your 401(k) has no surrender charges, but early withdrawal penalties and taxes can cost 30 to 50 percent.

- Your home has no surrender charges, but selling costs 6 to 8 percent in real estate agent fees and closing costs.

Every financial tool has costs. The question is whether the benefits justify them over time.

Objection #3: "Buy Term and Invest the Difference is Better."

The Truth: "Buy term and invest the difference" has been proven in multiple studies to be less effective than commonly believed. In fact, Ernst & Young, one of the Big Four global accounting firms, published an article on February 10th, 2021, titled "Benefits of Integrating Insurance Products into a Retirement Plan."

In their research, they compared five common retirement strategies to determine which provided the best overall results. Spoiler alert: It wasn't "Buy term and invest the difference."

If you'd like to read the full article, you can find it linked on the home page of my website: www.LegacyLifeandRetirement.com

Unfortunately, this remains one of the most popular pieces of financial advice circulating today—so let's take a closer, more critical look at it.

The Theory:

- Dave Ramsey is famous for telling his followers all they need to do is buy some cheap term insurance and then proceeds to send them to a company he financially benefits from that sells term.

- You're then instructed to invest the premium difference in mutual funds (Dave's suggested funds).

- And magically without question you'll come out ahead because of higher stock market returns—maybe.

Why it Usually Fails in Practice:

1. People Don't Actually Invest the Difference

Studies show that fewer than 5 percent of people who buy term life insurance actually invest the premium difference consistently. Most spend it. Human behavior is what it is.

2. Term Insurance Gets Expensive

Term premiums increase dramatically with age, and we all know people are living much longer these days. A policy that costs $500/year at age thirty might cost $4,000/year at age fifty and $8,000/year at age sixty, if you're still insurable. Not to mention that statistically speaking, less than 2 percent of term policies ever pay out a death benefit.

3. Market Timing Risk

This strategy assumes you'll retire during a market high. What if you retire during the next 2008-style crash? Your "investments" could be worth 40 to 50 percent less than expected. Timing matters, and you can't control it.

4. Tax Consequences

Investment gains are taxable. Policy loans are not. This difference compounds significantly over time.

Real-World Comparison: Let's compare two thirty-five-year-olds over thirty years:

Person A (Buy Term and Invest Difference):

- $200/month term premium (increasing with age)

- $800/month invested in mutual funds (assuming 8 percent "average" return)

- Total invested over thirty years: $360,000

- Market value at age sixty-five: $980,000 (before taxes)

- Life insurance at age sixty-five: Expired or unaffordable

Person B (Whole Life Strategy):

- $1,000/month whole life premium (level for life)

- Total contributed over thirty years: $360,000

- Cash value at age sixty-five: $640,000 (tax-free access via loans)

- Death benefit at age sixty-five: $1,325,000 (guaranteed, tax-free)

- Plus: Plus Person B had access to cash throughout the thirty years for opportunities

At first glance, Person A might seem wealthier. But once you factor in taxes, the loss of a death benefit, no creditor protection, zero access to living benefits if they become seriously ill, and a complete lack of liquidity during the accumulation years, the picture changes fast.

In reality, Person B holds the stronger position—more protected, more flexible, and better equipped for long-term security and growth.

Objection #4: "I'm Young and Healthy. I Don't Need Life Insurance."

The Truth: This is exactly when you *do* need life insurance, for reasons that have nothing to do with dying.

When You're Young:

- Premiums are at their lowest (and stay level for life).

- You're most likely to qualify for preferred rates (which means your dollar stretches further).

- You have the most time for cash value to compound (Success = Time x Uninterrupted Compounding).

- You can lock in insurability before health issues arise (meaning no matter what happens in the future you can still get coverage).

The Real Reasons Young People Should Consider Whole Life:

1. **Future Insurability:** Health can change overnight. Lock in coverage while you're healthy.

2. **Compound Growth:** Starting at twenty-five vs. thirty-five can mean hundreds of thousands more in cash value.

3. **Financial Flexibility:** Having liquid capital available for opportunities is valuable at any age.

4. **Debt Protection:** If you have student loans or other debts, life insurance can protect your co-signers by providing a death benefit that pays off those obligations if something happens to you.

Consider This: Every year you wait, the cost goes up and the potential accumulation goes down. As the old saying goes, "The best time to plant a tree was twenty years ago. The second-best time is now."

Objection #5: "I Can Get Better Returns Elsewhere."

The Truth: This objection misses the point entirely. Whole life insurance isn't about maximizing returns; it's about optimizing your entire financial system and putting the control back in your hands.

What "Better Returns" Usually Ignore:

- Taxes on those returns

- Volatility and timing risk

- Lack of liquidity during accumulation

- No death benefit protection

- No asset protection benefits

- No guaranteed growth

The Power of Multiple Benefits: A whole life policy giving you 4 to 5 percent might be better than a mutual fund giving you 8 percent because:

- The 4 to 5 percent is guaranteed and tax-advantaged.

- You can access it without penalty anytime.

- You can borrow against it while it keeps growing.

- It comes with death benefit protection.

- It provides asset protection in many states.

- It creates banking capabilities giving you the ability to grow your wealth while still funding your life.

Real Wealth Builders Think Differently: They don't just chase the highest return. They ask:

- How much control do I have?

- How liquid is my capital?

- What are the tax implications?

- How does this protect my downside?

- Can I use this for multiple purposes simultaneously?

Objection #6: "It's Too Complicated."

The Truth: The concept is simple—the industry and other talking heads trying to confuse you have made it seem complicated.

The Basic Concept:

1. Pay premiums into a policy.

2. Cash value grows guaranteed every year.

3. Borrow against your cash value when you need capital.

4. Repay loans on your timeline.

5. Pass death benefit to heirs tax-free.

What Makes it Seem Complicated:

- Insurance agents often use industry jargon instead of plain English.

- There are multiple policy types with similar but confusing names.

- Illustrations and projections can feel overwhelming, with too many numbers and scenarios.

- And, of course, the countless number of "experts" online trying to convince you it's some kind of investment—when it's not.

The Reality: Using a whole life policy for banking is simpler than:

- Managing a stock portfolio

- Understanding your 401(k) investment options

- Navigating real estate investments

- Running a business

Once you understand the basics, it becomes second nature.

Objection #7: "My Financial Advisor Says it's a Bad Idea."

The Truth: There's a strong chance that your current advisor knows very little—if anything—about properly structured whole life insurance. If they claim it's a "bad idea" or aren't suggesting you consider adding it to your portfolio, feel free to ask them exactly how it works and why they would claim it's a poor decision if Ernst & Young unbiasedly wrote about how it's a crucial part of a well rounded plan.

Why Many Advisors Oppose Whole Life Insurance:

1. Compensation Structure

Most financial advisors are paid through assets under management (AUM) fees. They earn ongoing fees on your mutual fund investments but only a one-time commission on insurance. If you were them, which would you prefer to recommend?

2. Training and Knowledge Gaps

Many advisors receive limited training on life insurance and have never studied the infinite banking concept. They're repeating what they've been taught, not what they've researched or personally utilized themselves.

3. Regulatory Environment

The securities industry has spent decades positioning insurance as "competition" rather than a complementary tool. Unfortunately, this creates built-in bias against insurance products when instead they should go hand in hand.

The Questions to Ask Your Advisor:

1. "How much life insurance do you personally own?"

2. "Have you studied the infinite banking concept specifically?"

3. "How are you compensated on insurance vs. investments?"

4. "Can you show me a client who successfully used 'buy term and invest the difference' for thirty-plus years?"

What Knowledgeable Advisors Say: Fee-only advisors and those who truly understand wealth building often recommend whole life insurance as part of a comprehensive strategy, especially for:

- High-income earners who've maxed out retirement accounts.

- Business owners needing liquidity and tax advantages.

- Families wanting to create generational wealth.

- People seeking guaranteed growth with upside potential and liquidity.

The Bottom Line: It's Not About Perfect; It's About Control.

Whole life insurance isn't perfect—no financial tool is. But it's one of the few tools that gives you:

- Guaranteed growth every year.

- Tax advantages that work in your favor.

- Liquidity without penalties or restrictions.

- Death benefit protection for your family.

- Asset protection benefits.

- Banking capabilities.

It's not whether whole life insurance is the "best investment" (because it's not an investment). The real question is: Does it make your overall financial plan stronger, safer, and more flexible?

For most people building wealth outside the traditional system, the answer is yes.

Moving Forward

If you've made it this far, you've already cleared the biggest hurdle—realizing that **whole life insurance isn't the problem**; it's the misunderstanding around how it's used. When structured properly, it's not just a policy—it's a financial foundation.

The objections we've covered aren't *wrong*—they're just **incomplete**. They focus on what this strategy *can't* do, without recognizing what it *can*. They compare it to the wrong tools and assume you're chasing the highest return, instead of the highest level of **control, flexibility, and long-term certainty**.

Now that you understand how the system really works—and how the wealthy have quietly been using it for generations—it's time to take the next step. In the next chapter, we'll shift from understanding the concept to **becoming the bank**.

Because once you start seeing yourself as the bank, everything about how you build, protect, and grow your wealth changes.

CHAPTER 10

Your New Identity— You're the Bank Now

"The cave you fear to enter holds the treasure you seek." - Joseph Campbell

By this point, you should have a clear understanding of how banks operate. You've learned the limitations of traditional financial strategies and you've discovered the power of strategic compounding. In the following section, we'll dive deep into multiple examples of how to put your capital to work using OPM without giving up control. Information alone, however, doesn't change lives. Action does. And sustainable action comes from the identity you've built for yourself. It's about who you believe you can be now with the knowledge you've gained.

You are not just a consumer anymore. You are not just a saver. You are not just a borrower. You are the banker, and the banker is in control.

I can teach you every strategy in this book, but if you don't change how you see yourself, you'll eventually drift back to old patterns. That's human nature.

The people who succeed long term with this approach don't just learn the techniques—they adopt a new identity. They stop thinking like customers and start thinking like owners. They stop reacting to financial circumstances and start creating them. This isn't just about money; it's about taking control of your life in a way that most people never do.

The Banking Mindset: How the Wealthy Really Think

Banks don't hope for good returns—they create systems that generate predictable returns. They don't worry about market volatility—they build diversified income streams. They don't chase the latest investment fad—they stick to proven principles that have worked for decades.

When you adopt the banking mindset, you start asking different questions:

Instead of: "How can I get a higher return?"

Ask: "How can I create more control?"

Instead of: "What's the best investment right now?"

Ask: "How can I build a system that works in any market?"

Instead of: "Should I pay off debt or invest?"

Ask: "How can I pay off debt AND invest simultaneously?"

This shift in thinking is what separates wealth builders from wealth daydreamers.

Let me show you why thinking like a bank works so well. "According to the Federal Deposit Insurance Corporation (FDIC), the U.S. banking industry reported net income of $268.2 billion in 2024."[14] That's not because they got lucky or timed the market perfectly; it's because they follow consistent principles:

1. They Control the Spread

Banks consistently earn 3 to 4 percent on the difference between what they pay depositors and what they charge borrowers. It's not spectacular, but it's predictable and scalable.

2. They Diversify Income Streams

Banks don't rely on just one source of income. They have:

- Net interest income (lending spreads).

- Fee income (services, transactions).

- Investment income (securities).

- Trading income (market activities).

3. They Maintain Liquidity

Banks keep enough cash accessible to meet daily operations while putting the rest to work. They never trap all their capital in illiquid investments.

4. They Think Long Term

Banks don't panic during market downturns. They maintain their core operations and often increase market share when competitors struggle.

---

14   Federal Deposit Insurance Corporation (FDIC). *Quarterly Banking Profile: Fourth Quarter 2024*. Washington, D.C.: FDIC, 2025. Available at: https://www.fdic.gov/analysis/quarterly-banking-profile/

When you apply those same principles to your personal finances, you get similar results: predictable growth, multiple income streams, maintained liquidity, and long-term wealth building.

The Confidence to Lead Your Family's Financial Future

You might be the first in your family to do this. You might be the only one in your friend group not maxing out a 401(k). You might feel like you're swimming upstream at times.

Good. That's exactly how you know you're on the right path.

The people who change the direction of their family's financial history don't follow the crowd; they lead it. And leading requires belief. You have to believe:

- That you are worth building wealth for.

- That your children deserve better than the financial stress you may have experienced.

- That your future is worth funding with intention, not hope.

- That you can learn to do things differently than you were taught.

When you adopt this new identity, you begin to see every financial decision through a different lens: "Would a bank do this?" If the answer is no, maybe you shouldn't either.

The Ripple Effect: How Your Identity Shift Affects Everything

When you truly adopt the banker identity, it doesn't just change how you handle money; it changes how you approach everything.

Your Career: You start seeing your job as one income stream among many, not your only source of financial security.

Your Relationships: You begin having different conversations with your spouse and children about money, teaching them to think like owners rather than consumers.

Your Decisions: You evaluate opportunities based on cash flow and control rather than just potential returns.

Your Legacy: You start building something that will outlast you, not just accumulating assets for retirement.

Your Confidence: You stop worrying about market crashes and economic uncertainty because you've built a system that works in any environment.

Guiding Practices

Identity is reinforced through consistently repeated actions. Here are the practices that successful family bankers incorporate into their routine:

Weekly Banking Review (thirty minutes):

- Check policy cash values and loan balances.

- Analyze cash flow from all sources.

- Evaluate any new investment opportunities.

- Plan next moves for capital deployment.

Each week, I set aside about thirty minutes for what I call my Weekly Banking Review. During that time, I check the cash values and loan balances on my policies to make sure everything is growing as expected and that I have a clear picture of my available capital. I also take a quick look at my overall cash flow—what's coming in, what's going out, and where I might be able to redirect dollars more efficiently. From there, I review any new investment opportunities that have come up during the week and decide whether it makes sense to deploy capital or let it continue compounding inside my system. Finally, I plan my next moves—whether that's repaying a policy loan, funding a new asset, or simply letting my reserves build for the next opportunity. Doing this once a week keeps me connected to my system and ensures that every dollar I earn continues working for me, instead of sitting idle.

Monthly Strategic Planning (sixty minutes):

- Review all income streams and investments.

- Assess progress toward financial goals.

- Plan next quarter's capital allocation.

Once a month, I dedicate about an hour to what I call Monthly Strategic Planning. This is where I zoom out and look at the bigger picture—reviewing all of my income streams, current investments, and how they're performing. I assess where I stand in relation to my financial goals and identify any adjustments I need to make. From there, I map out my plan for the next quarter—deciding how and where I want to allocate capital to keep my system growing efficiently and in alignment with my long-term vision.

Quarterly System Optimization:

- Meet with your team (IBC practitioner, CPA, etc.).

- Review and adjust strategy based on results.

- Plan the next phase of income stacking or system expansion.

Every quarter, I schedule time for what I call System Optimization. For you, this is when I would suggest meeting with your team—your infinite banking practitioner, CPA, and anyone else involved in your financial strategy—to review performance and results from the past few months. When meeting with my team, this is when we look for ways to fine-tune the system, adjust cash flow strategies, and identify new opportunities for growth. From there, I plan the next phase of income stacking or system expansion, ensuring that every part of my financial engine continues running efficiently and in sync with my long-term goals.

These aren't just financial activities; they're identity reinforcement practices. Each time you do them, you're strengthening your identity as someone who controls their financial destiny.

When I think back to where I was before all of this, it's hard to believe how much has changed. Like you, I was working hard, saving what I could and trying to do everything "right"—but I still felt like I was spinning my wheels, getting absolutely nowhere. Money came in and went right back out. I didn't have control. What I did have was confusion, stress, and a lot of misplaced hope that someday, it would all just work out.

I attribute where I am today to the massive mindset shift I had years ago. I stopped doing a lot of the things that weren't moving me forward and instead started studying real financial principles, attending events, and working with mentors who showed me how to build my own family banking system. The first time I realized my money could grow uninterrupted and still be used at the same time—something clicked. I stopped seeing money as something I had to chase and started seeing it as something I could command.

Now, I move through life with purpose and peace. My dollars have direction, my decisions have meaning, and my family's future is built on a foundation I control. In a matter of five short years, we went from being $60,000 in debt to building almost $100,000 a year in passive income. The crazy part is this is just the beginning. Becoming my own banker didn't just change my finances—it completely shifted my mindset, rebuilt my belief system, and opened a door to generational wealth I never thought was possible for a regular guy like me. In Chapter 11, I'll break down some of the financial moves we made that allowed us to start building massive momentum.

Final Word: This is Just the Beginning

The purpose of this chapter isn't to convince you that you've "arrived." You haven't. None of us have. Building wealth is a lifelong journey, and adopting the banker identity is just the foundation. It just happens to be the most important foundation you can build.

From here, you'll continue refining your system. You'll find better investments, build stronger habits, and surround yourself with mentors and communities who support your growth.

You now have knowledge that most people don't. You have tools that most people will never learn to use. You have the ability to create financial freedom for your family. What you do with that knowledge, tools, and ability is up to you.

It's time to move from Step Two to Step Three as we shift our focus from building our system to multiplying our income. In the next chapter, we'll dive into exactly how to put this tool to work through the power of Other People's Money, showing you how to use your policy as the foundation for building multiple income streams while your capital continues to grow uninterrupted.

"The significant problems we face cannot be solved at the same level of thinking we were at when we created them." - Albert Einstein

It's time to think differently about your money.

THE INCOME MULTIPLIER

CHAPTER 11

The Power of OPM

By this point, we've covered a lot of ground. You understand the mindset shift of becoming your own banker, you know how to build your Warehouse of Wealth, and we've tackled the biggest objections head-on.

Now let's get to the fun part: putting your system to work.

This is where Other People's Money (OPM) makes the strategy come alive. Your policy is growing. Your life is protected. Now we put the engine in gear and start building multiple income streams that can take you *From Regular to Rich.*

Why Early Policy Years Feel "Heavy" (and How to Accelerate)

Think of a properly structured whole life policy like an airplane's fuel consumption. Planes burn more fuel during takeoff because a full tank is heavy. As fuel gets consumed, the plane becomes lighter, and efficiency improves.

Your banking system works in a similar way. When your policy first begins, you have the death benefit that protects your life, but what you don't have is access to every dollar you put in to borrow against. Like I mentioned in the previous chapter, this takes a little time to build up. However, with the Paid-Up Additions rider added on, you can significantly accelerate your cash value growth.

By contributing PUAs each year, you're essentially putting more fuel in the tank faster, which gives you more borrowing power sooner. In a typical scenario, you might have access to 90 percent of your cash value within the first thirty days through policy loans.

Here's where it gets interesting: Once you have usable cash value, you can start implementing what we call income stacking. Income stacking is the systematic use of policy loans to create multiple income streams that fund future policies and investments.

The Mindset of OPM

When people hear "Other People's Money," they often think of mega-developers or Wall Street traders, but OPM isn't some insider game reserved for the ultra-wealthy.

Once you understand how to leverage your own cash value, OPM becomes a tool for everyday wealth builders like us. The beauty is you're not starting from scratch or begging banks for loans. You're starting from a position of strength because your Warehouse of Wealth is already growing behind the scenes.

Banks have always understood the power of using Other People's Money. They don't withdraw their own reserves when they issue loans; they keep their money growing and leverage yours. By putting OPM to work through your own system, you step into the most powerful position in finance: the banker.

Real-World Investment Strategies: Building Passive Income Streams

Below are several strategies I've used personally, along with many of my clients, to create cash flow and multiply returns using policy loans. I included realistic return expectations, risk management tips, and common mistakes to avoid.

Remember, there are countless ways to invest outside the stock market, but here's the key: If it's not something you're genuinely interested in, there's a good chance it won't work out. Pick strategies that align with your interests and expertise.

Disclaimer: The information provided here is for educational purposes only. Any financial decisions you make should be based on your own research, due diligence, and consideration of your personal circumstances.

1. Private Lending with Real Estate Investors

This is one of my favorite cash flow strategies because it's predictable, consistent, and can be secured with real assets. You loan capital from your policy to vetted real estate investors who need short-term funding for flips, rehabs, or land development.

Typical Structure:

- Loan term: six to twelve months (often interest-only)

- Typical returns: 10 to 18 percent annualized

- Security: first-position lien on the property (meaning if the borrower defaults on their payments, you have legal claim to take ownership of the property)

According to ATTOM Data Solutions, there were over 407,000 house flips in the U.S. in 2023, representing 8.4 percent of all home sales. The average gross profit per flip was $66,300. This creates consistent demand for short-term lending capital.[15]

Example:

Let's say we loan $100,000 at 12 percent interest for twelve months.

- Annual cash flow: $12,000/year + growth within policy (guarantees + dividends)

- Return of 100K investment at the end of the twelve-month term.

Risk Management Tips:

- Always vet the borrower's experience and track record.

- Confirm the property's value supports your lien amount.

- Get everything in writing, including repayment schedule and default terms.

- Never lend more than 70 percent of the property value.

Platforms like PrivateMoneyClub.com connect people with capital to those who need it. Think of it as a dating site for borrowers and lenders. It's free to set up a profile and explore available opportunities.

---

15   ATTOM Data Solutions. *U.S. Home Flipping Report – Year-End 2023*. Irvine, CA: ATTOM, 2024. Available at: https://www.attomdata.com/news/market-trends/home-flipping/year-end-2023-u-s-home-flipping-report/

2. Income Stacking Through Private Lending Networks

While private lending on real estate flips focuses on short-term, higher-interest loans to active investors, there's another strategy that I personally utilize that emphasizes building multiple passive income streams systematically over time.

If you're ready to move beyond single-deal lending and you have access to a modest amount of capital, private lending networks and note marketplaces offer a fundamentally different approach to leveraging your infinite banking system.

Instead of you having to find a borrower, underwrite the deal, service the loan, and collect payments yourself, these platforms act as infrastructure. They can give you access to mortgage notes and peer-to-peer lending opportunities where cash flow comes back in monthly payments—exactly where the concept of income stacking shines. As author Michael Kwong explains in his book DIBS On Your Money!, income stacking isn't just about having multiple income streams; it's about strategically layering those streams so they compound and accelerate your wealth-building velocity. When it comes to income stacking, it's not about the rate (the percentage you're earning); it's about volume (the number of income streams you're creating).

Why I like this approach:

- **Built to stack:** Many of these investments are structured around monthly payments, which makes them easy to "layer" over time instead of relying on one big home run.

- **Reasonable entry points:** In many cases you can start small and scale. For example, Prosper's stated minimum investment for an individual general investment account is $25. Groundfloor states you can start investing with as little as $100.

- **Clear mechanics:** You invest in notes/loans, payments come in, and the platform handles the payment processing and servicing.

- **Real-world exposure:** Depending on the platform, you may be investing in real estate-backed debt (secured by property) or consumer loans (tied to borrower repayment).

- **Strong synergy with your system:** This strategy pairs well with policy loans because you can deploy capital and control the repayment schedule all while your cash value continues compounding in the background—the velocity component at work.

How the stacking works (generalized):

You take a policy loan to fund your first income-producing note or lending position. That investment begins generating monthly payments in most cases (principal plus interest). You combine those payments with your freed-up cash flow and repay your policy loan on an accelerated schedule that fits your household. Once the policy loan is repaid, you're still receiving payments from that original investment for the remainder of its term. That new cash flow can then help fund the next stack.

Then you repeat: you take a new loan for an equal or larger amount, add the ongoing passive income from the first stack to your available cash flow, and pay the second stack down on an accelerated timeline. Now you've layered two income streams, offset in time, each producing monthly payments. Over time, the "payoff window" can shrink because your existing passive income is helping carry the next stack. When you can comfortably recycle capital faster, that's when it makes sense to scale the size of the next stack.

Also important: terms vary. Some notes or loans may run 12 months, others 36 months, and some longer. Some will kick back 4-5% interest while others are 10-12%. The point isn't to chase one perfect term—it's to build a repeatable system that adds another payment stream on top of the last one.

A quick word on risk: none of these are "guaranteed," even when they're tied to real assets. Borrowers can default. Real estate values can change. Some investments may be illiquid until the note is paid off, and platforms have their own operational risks. And let me be clear—"asset-backed" doesn't mean "risk-free."

The solution isn't fear, it's discipline. Start smaller than you think you need to. Diversify across multiple notes or loans instead of concentrating on just one. Read how the platform handles late payments, defaults, and workouts. Know whether you can exit early or you're committed to the term. And when you're using a policy loan as your funding source, choose a repayment pace your household can sustain even if a payment comes in late or a deal takes longer than expected to perform.

Where to start researching (not endorsements—just strong starting points)

1. **Mortgage note marketplace / transaction infrastructure**

   Paperstac positions itself as a digital mortgage note transaction engine—essentially a marketplace + closing process for buying and selling mortgage notes. (Paperstac.com)

2. **Peer-to-peer consumer lending (invest in notes tied to borrower loans)**

   Prosper is a lending marketplace where investors invest in "notes" (or portions) of borrower loans, and Prosper's payments to investors are dependent on borrower payments. (Prosper.com/invest)

3. **Real estate debt investing (fractional access to real estate-backed lending)**

   Groundfloor states you can start investing with as little as $100 and frames the offering around real estate investing without directly buying property. (Groundfloor.com)

Strategy:

Let's say you decide to start investing with Prosper. For this example let's say you invest $10,000 funded by a policy loan and you're earning 12% APY. As monthly payments come in (approx $332/m), use that cash plus your freed-up monthly cash flow ($2,000 in this scenario) to repay your policy over the next four to five months before paying off your original note and starting a "new stack". In the first year alone, you should be able to create three to four notes each paying you $332 a month before increasing your stack size when appropriate. The goal is to not touch the income being generated from the notes for the first three years, but instead continue to pay off your individual note, then reinvest in a new larger note creating an even larger kickback in passive income. Don't forget all of this is happening while your policy's cash value continues growing in the background, tax-free. Below I've laid out exactly what your first four stacks would look like by using the numbers listed above. At the end of stack four, you would have been stacking for just over a year. If you were to remove your $2,000 of personal income from the equation at that point, you would have created approximately $1,328 a month of passive income. The longer you stack, the more drastically that number begins to increase. Much like the growth curve in your whole life policy. Remember it's not about rate, it's about volume.

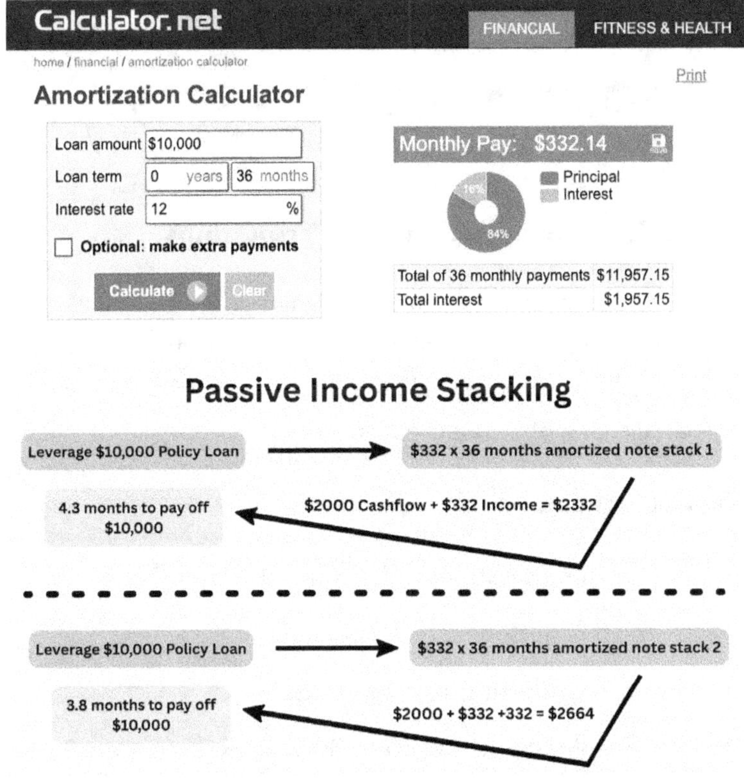

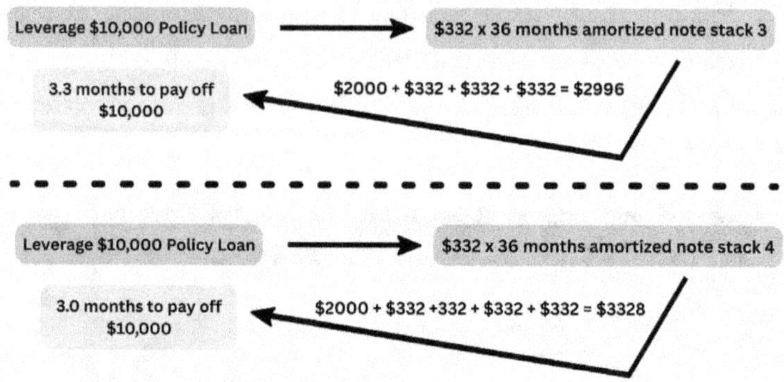

3. Real Estate Syndications and Partnerships

Not everyone wants to be a landlord or manage tenants. That's why, oftentimes, investors may look to real estate syndications. These are professionally managed pooled investments in apartment complexes, self-storage, or mobile home parks.

Typical Structure:

- Minimum investment: $25,000 to $100,000

- Annual cash flow: 6 to 10 percent

- Hold period: three to seven years

- Profit split at sale: 70/30 or 80/20 (investor/sponsor)

- Tax advantages: Depreciation can offset income.

The National Multifamily Housing Council reports that institutional investment in multifamily properties reached $202 billion in 2023. This includes syndications accessible to accredited investors.[16]

Example:

If you invest $50,000 from a policy loan into a syndication paying 8 percent annually:

- Annual cash flow: $4,000/year + growth within policy (guarantees + dividends)

- Plus potential profit at sale in five to seven years

When first getting started, be sure to only work with operators who have successfully managed multiple projects through full cycles. Understand the local market and property fundamentals. Review their track record of distributions and investor communication.

4. Low Stress Options: How I Learned to Create Weekly Cashflow With Puts and Calls (Without Living on a Screen)

You and I both know if you're going to build wealth, at some point you're going to need to invest. Nothing outside of your family banking system is guaranteed—but the life you want will require you to take risks somewhere. The real question is: what risks are you taking, and how much control do you have over them? For me, learning "low stress options" was one of those things that changed my financial life in a very practical way.

Before this, I knew nothing about calls or puts. Literally zero. It sounded like something Wall Street guys did in dark rooms with

---

16   National Multifamily Housing Council (NMHC) *NMHC Quarterly Survey of Apartment Market Conditions – Q4 2023*. Washington, D.C.: National Multifamily Housing Council, 2024. Available at: https://www.nmhc.org/research-insight/quarterly-survey-of-apartment-market-conditions/

three monitors and a little something extra to keep them going. I've got to be honest though, once I learned the process—and more importantly, the risk controls—it became simple. And that's what I want to share with you: not hype, not theory, just something that has worked for a regular guy and his family.

What this actually is (and what it is NOT)

Let me be clear. This is not day trading. This isn't buying options and hoping for a big move. This isn't using margin or leverage, and it's not gambling. The "low stress" approach is built around selling option premium with collateral using two basic tools:

1) Cash-Secured Puts

2) Covered Calls.

That's it.

Selling premium means you're getting paid up front for agreeing to buy or sell an asset at a pre-decided price. Think of options like insurance. In this scenario you're selling the insurance, getting paid up front, and using a specific set of rules so the risk stays controlled.

Here's how it works in plain English:

Step 1: Choose an asset/stock you would actually be willing to own. Because sometimes you will end up owning it. That's just part of the strategy.

Step 2: Sell a cash-secured put. This means you hold the cash needed to buy 100 shares at a specific price (the strike). You collect a premium immediately.

Two outcomes:

A) If the price stays above your strike, you keep the premium and keep your cash.

B) If the price drops below your strike, you may get assigned—meaning you buy the shares at the strike price (and your effective price is reduced because you already got paid premium).

Step 3: If assigned, sell a covered call. Now that you own the shares, you sell a call contract against them. You collect a premium again.

Two outcomes:

A) If the price stays below your call strike, you keep the premium and keep the shares.

B) If the price rises above your call strike, your shares may get called away and you go back to cash. Then you repeat.

Cash → sell puts → (sometimes buy shares) → sell calls → back to cash.

I'm not a big fan of investing in the stock market but this works for a few very specific reasons: It requires minimal time, there's very clear and easy rules to follow, there's no middle man you have to worry might mess the deal up.

Here's what surprised me: Once you understand how it works, it doesn't take much time. I'm not managing this all day. I'm definitely not staring at charts, and I'm not checking my phone every five minutes. Most weeks, it's about an hour of focused time to place trades, adjust if needed, and move on. That's part of why it fits my lifestyle. It's structured. It's repeatable. And it doesn't require me to be "right" about the market every day.

Low Stress Trading promotes 1% a week (my real experience)

You'll hear the founders of Low Stress Trading talk about targeting 1% gains a week which seems insane if you think about it. I'm going to be honest: when done correctly, with the proper risk mitigation in place and the process followed, that's been a realistic average for myself and for many others who operate within this framework. Is it guaranteed? No. Will every single week look like 1%? Of course not.

There will be weeks where premiums are smaller because volatility is low. There will be times you get assigned and you're holding shares longer than expected. There will be moments where the market moves fast and you have to follow your rules instead of your emotions. But the reason the 1% idea is powerful is because it's not based on prediction. It's based on process. And compounding small, repeatable wins—when managed correctly—adds up.

Like any investment this isn't meant to replace your family banking system. Your policy gives you liquidity and control—so you can invest without being forced into bad decisions. This is simply one more tool you can choose to learn. Maybe it fits you. Maybe it doesn't. But I'd rather you be educated on what exists than trapped in the default plan because nobody ever showed you alternatives. All of these investment strategies are worth looking into but only you can decide which strategy will best fit your investment style. Below I have included a snapshot from an investment calculator Low Stress Trading provides on their website. The example is for a five year period starting with a $10,000 investment adding an additional $100 every month earning their estimated 1% weekly projected earnings.

Weekly Return	Starting Balance	Weekly Extra
1%	$10,000	$100

Year	Starting Balance	Total Contribution	Ending Balance	Monthly Income
1	$10,000.00	$5,200.00	$23,553.78	$1,020.66
2	$23,553.78	$10,400.00	$46,292.80	$2,006.02
3	$46,292.80	$15,600.00	$84,441.81	$3,659.15
4	$84,441.81	$20,800.00	$148,443.98	$6,432.57
5	$148,443.98	$26,000.00	$255,819.71	$11,085.52

If you want to learn more about the company that teaches this strategy or try out the calendar visit: https://lowstresstrading.com/options?ref=Legacy

These are just a few of my favorite ways to leverage our system and build the passive income needed to fund my family's travel lifestyle. I didn't want the normal nine-to-five; I wanted freedom. These investments allowed me to grow my wealth without sacrificing time or energy, all with the goal of reaching my freedom number.

The Psychology of Using OPM

Here's something most people don't understand about using Other People's Money effectively: It's not just about the mechanics; it's about the mindset.

People who successful use OPM think differently:

- They see money as a tool, not a scorecard.

- They focus on cash flow, not just appreciation.

- They understand that velocity creates wealth.

- They're comfortable with strategic debt when properly collateralized.

When you know you have accessible capital in your policies, you're not desperate to chase returns. You can afford to be selective, which usually leads to better decisions and higher-quality opportunities.

Traditional investing often means giving up control for potentially higher returns. With the private banking system, you maintain control of your base capital while using policy loans to access opportunities. If an investment doesn't work out, which can definitely happen, at least you have the peace of mind knowing that the cash in your policy continues growing, uninterrupted.

Why This Works: Cash Flow and Control

The beauty of this strategy is elegantly simple: You never give up control of your money.

You're not waiting for a retirement date. You're not hoping a stock market recovery bails you out. You're moving money through your private system, giving every dollar the ability to work in multiple places simultaneously.

Here's what that looks like in practice:

1. Your money earns uninterrupted compound growth in the policy.

2. You access capital through policy loans (no disruption to growth).

3. You deploy that capital into cash-flowing assets.

4. You repay policy loans from your cash flow with interest, giving you access to those dollars again.

5. You rinse and repeat, increasing your wealth each time.

That's strategic compounding and OPM working together. You're not waiting for financial freedom; you're building it in real time.

One often overlooked benefit of building your own banking system: It gives you the power to say yes to the right opportunities and no to the wrong ones.

If a deal doesn't meet your criteria, whether it's too risky, too slow, or doesn't align with your values, you can pass without stress. You're not desperate to chase returns because your core system is already growing steadily.

But when a great opportunity shows up, you have capital ready to deploy. No applications. No waiting for approval. No worrying about market timing. Just access.

That's what real wealth provides. It's not just a number on a screen; it's the confidence to act and the freedom to walk away.

You Don't Have to Be Rich to Start

The beautiful thing about private lending and income stacking is that it scales with your capital. You don't need huge amounts to begin.

Start Small:

- Open an account with Groundfloor or a similar P2P platform like Prosper.

- Join vetted real estate groups or communities revolving around your interest.

- Surround yourself with people already doing what you want to do.

- Start with what you can afford to lose while you learn.

Build Systematically:

- Use small wins to build confidence and capital.

- Reinvest returns into additional policies and opportunities.

- Focus on cash flow first, appreciation second.

- Learn from every experience, successful or not.

Every time you successfully deploy capital and generate returns, you're taking one step closer to true financial independence. You're activating your system, deploying OPM, and multiplying the work each dollar can do.

Note: All investment examples are for educational purposes. Returns are not guaranteed, and all investments carry risk. Consult with qualified professionals before making any investment decisions.

You've now learned how to put your money to work using leverage, policy loans, and the power of Other People's Money to create real, usable cash flow. But building wealth is only half the battle—the other half is learning how to keep it. The most successful people I've met don't just focus on making money; they focus on keeping more of what they earn through smart, legal, and proactive strategies. In the next chapter, we're going to talk about exactly that—how to shift from being a taxpayer to a tax planner. Because if you're serious about living freely and building generational wealth, you have to master both sides of the equation: cash flow and control.

CHAPTER 12

The Truth About Taxes

"It's not how much money you make. It's how much money you keep." – Robert Kiyosaki

Look, I'm gonna be straight with you—you should be very interested in learning how to legally *not* pay taxes. But there's a huge difference between reducing taxes and evading them. One saves you money; the other gets you about twenty-five years in an orange jumpsuit, and that's not the kind of lifestyle upgrade we're going for.

Here's the thing that drives me nuts: Taxes are probably one of the biggest expenses you'll face in your entire life, but most of us just ignore them. We act like they're this unchangeable force of nature, such as the weather or gravity. That's exactly how the system wants you to think so you continue to blindly give them more of your money than necessary.

Let me be clear from the start—I'm not a CPA, and I'm not pretending to be one. What I am is someone who got tired of getting blindsided by taxes every year and decided to do something about it. I built a proactive team of professionals around me who helped myself and my clients navigate the tax code *before* it was too late to change anything.

In this chapter, I'm going to show you some strategies you can start using right now so you can stop dreading tax season and start making it work for you instead. The wealthy in this country have been taking advantage of this for decades. Somehow the rest of us never got the memo. Well, consider this your memo.

The Problem: Defense vs. Offense

You've heard the saying about death and taxes being the only certainties in life, right? Well, here's what they don't tell you: You actually get to decide how much you pay in taxes based on how well you plan for them.

Most people think about taxes exactly once a year, when their accountant calls (if they even have an accountant) and tells them what they owe. By then, it's game over. That's like trying to win a basketball game but not taking a shot until after the final buzzer. Sorry, the game's over. You lost.

Here's the real problem: We don't just need accountants; we need tax strategists. There's a big difference.

The IRS tax code is over 70,000 pages long. Let that sink in for a second. Buried in that mountain of bureaucratic fun are thousands of strategies for reducing your tax liability. Unfortunately, most of those strategies don't apply to W2 employees. They're written to benefit business owners, investors, and people who know how to play the game strategically.

So what does that mean for you? Find something you love doing—or, hell, something you're just decent at—and create a business out of it. Even if it's small. Even if it's just a side hustle, find out how to get a rental property or two because that's your ticket to play the game.

Be the Business

Your tax bill is shaped by the choices you make all year, not by what happens in March. One of the simplest moves? Operate like a business instead of taking every dollar as personal income. The tax code rewards owners and investors because they create jobs and activity. If you're W-2 only, options are tighter, but if you freelance, consult, run a side hustle, or invest in real estate, this can save you real money over time.

Pick a structure that fits your goals:

- **LLC (Limited Liability Company)**

  Easy to set up. Separates your business from your personal life, which helps protect your house, car, and savings if something goes wrong. They're flexible for taxes too; you can keep it as a disregarded entity or elect a different treatment later if it benefits you.

- **S Corporation (when it truly fits)**

  You pay yourself a reasonable salary (subject to payroll taxes) and can take the remaining profit as distributions that aren't hit with self-employment tax. Quick example: If your business nets $100,000, part becomes W-2 wages and part will be distributions. How you split it depends on your role and what's considered "reasonable." Run through this with a good CPA to make sure you're compliant.

An S corp is worth considering when you have consistent profits beyond what a reasonable salary would be for your role. If you're just starting or profits are inconsistent, stick with an LLC until the numbers justify the added complexity.

After you've chosen your structure, run it like a real business:

- **Keep finances separate** - Open a dedicated business bank account and maintain clean, organized books.

- **Track every deductible expense** - Record software, marketing, travel, mileage, and meals that qualify as business-related.

- **Create a simple reimbursement system** - Use an accountable plan, save receipts, and jot brief notes on each purchase for clarity at tax time.

- **Plan ahead for taxes** - Set aside money and review quarterly estimates so tax season never catches you off guard.

Bottom line: Structure creates options for liability protection, cash flow management, and tax efficiency. Set it up right, run it clean, and let the tax code work for you.

When you operate like a real business, you unlock benefits employees simply don't get. Since we're big fans of building passive income through real estate, let's talk about property-related tax strategies.

Property Savings (Simple, High-Impact)

If you run a business out of a home office, part of your real costs—internet, utilities, a portion of rent or mortgage, and office equipment—can count as business expenses. As long as you document these properly come tax season, these expenses will lower the income you're taxed on.

There's also a powerful, little-known rule my wife and I have used multiple times.

The "Augusta Rule" (IRC §280A(g)), in Plain English

Your company can rent your home or vacation property for short, legitimate business events, team meetings, client workshops, or content creation for up to fourteen days per year at fair market rates. We host our family banking and financial planning meetings at our home and take full advantage of this strategy.

Here's how it works:

- The business deducts the rent (just like paying for a hotel or coworking space).

- You don't report that rent as personal income (within the fourteen-day limit).

- Works best when your business is a separate entity (LLC/S corp), not a sole proprietorship.

Quick example: If similar spaces near you rent for $1,000 per day and you host one legitimate business event at your home each month, that's $12,000 deducted by the business and income you don't have to report personally.

Do it right (documentation matters):

- Put the event on your calendar with a brief agenda.

- Take photos or screenshots of the meeting setup.

- Create a simple invoice from you (homeowner) to your company.

- Use a reasonable market rate (research local venue pricing).

That's it: clean, simple, and completely legitimate. Small strategies like this put real dollars back in your pocket that you can reinvest into building wealth.

Note: Confirm details about entity type, fair market rates, and documentation requirements with your CPA.

Business Write-Offs (Keep What Grows the Business)

Here's the simple rule: If it helps you earn, maintain, or grow revenue, it might be a business expense. Employees don't get this flexibility, but business owners do. Your job is to keep it honest and keep it documented.

What typically counts:

- **Operations:** Software, subscriptions, phone, internet, office supplies.

- **Marketing and sales:** Advertising, design, video equipment, contractors, business gifts (within limits).

- **Travel and mileage:** Trips with legitimate business purposes, local driving for work.

- **Meals:** Business meetings and discussions (usually 50 percent deductible).

- **Education:** Courses and workshops that improve skills relevant to your business.

Make documentation effortless (your one-minute system):

- Use one business card or account. Keep personal expenses separate.

- Take a photo of receipts and add a brief note: "Lunch, client meeting with Alex about Q4 strategy."

- Keep a simple mileage log (use an app or calendar).

- Do a monthly review: categorize expenses, file receipts, done.

Important note: A deduction reduces taxable income—it's not free money. A $100 deductible expense doesn't put $100 back in your pocket; it saves you your tax rate on that $100. So be smart: Only spend money on what actually helps the business grow. See chart below for 2025 and 2026 Federal Income Tax Brackets.

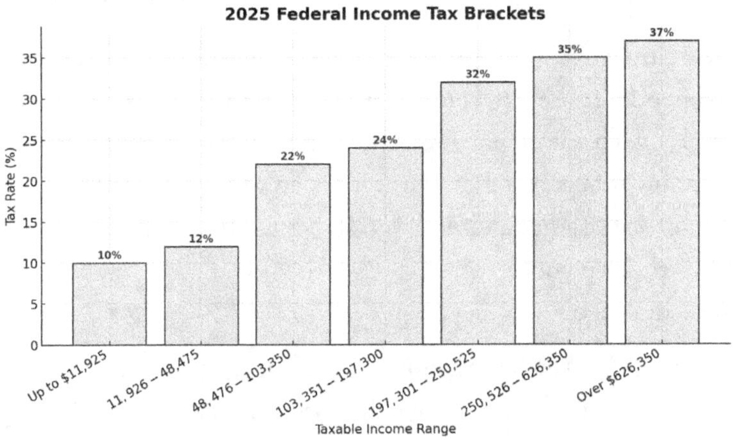

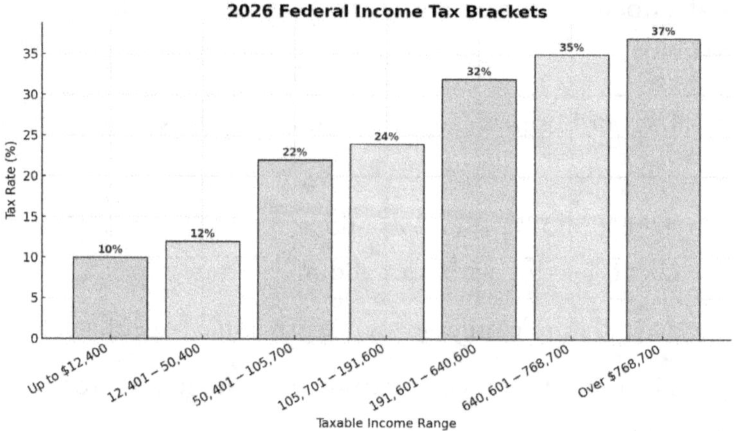

Depreciation

Everything you use to run your business wears out over time. Laptops slow down, phones break, chairs fall apart, and cameras lose their edge. The tax code recognizes this reality and lets you recover the cost of those tools gradually. That recovery is called depreciation.

Here's the basic concept: Instead of deducting the full cost of a business asset the day you buy it, you spread that cost across the years you'll use it. In practice, your CPA may accelerate some items and slow others based on current tax law, but you don't need to memorize the schedules. Your job is to buy what the business truly requires, keep good records, and let the system give you credit as those tools age.

Start simple. If you buy a laptop, desk, or camera you actually use for business, most of that cost can reduce your taxable income. Nothing lasts forever, and the tax code acknowledges that reality.

This same principle can scale up significantly. For example, vehicles used for business can be depreciated, and rental real estate uses depreciation strategies too. That's where things get interesting. A rental property can generate monthly cash flow while simultaneously "wearing out" on paper. The result? Your taxable income can be lower than your actual cash flow.

This is one reason some of the wealthiest business owners appear to pay very little in taxes. They're using assets that generate cash while also creating legitimate depreciation deductions.

You don't need a million-dollar apartment building to benefit from this. You can start with a single rental property that provides cash flow. Over time, as you grow your portfolio, a good CPA can help you use these strategies more efficiently.

The fundamentals don't change: Buy productive assets, keep clean books, and let depreciation work in the background.

One important caution: Don't buy things just for the tax write-off. A deduction only helps if the purchase genuinely helps the business. Cash flow first, tax benefits second. When you start combining both effectively, you'll quickly find yourself on the road *From Regular to Rich*.

Keep the Money in the Family

This strategy could change between now and when you're reading this, but paying your children for legitimate work is another way to keep more money in the family while reducing your tax burden. Be sure to check current regulations when you implement this.

Currently, the U.S. government allows for a standard deduction for taxpayers. This means up to that amount, a person may owe little to no federal income tax on earned wages.

Say the standard deduction for 2025 is $15,750 per year, meaning $0 in federal taxes need to be paid on the first $15,750 a taxpayer makes. If this is the case, you can pay your kids up to $15,750 per year to work within your business tax-free. You might be thinking to yourself, *Well, how does this help me?*

All the money you spend on school trips, sports, and activities can now come from their account. Your business deducts the wages (lowering your taxable income) while your kids don't pay federal taxes on money they earned from actual work. This means you effectively have more purchasing power for expenses you were already covering.

This is also a valuable opportunity to teach your kids about personal finance and work ethic.

When they realize it's their money being spent on new basketball shoes or gymnastics classes, it creates a whole new sense of responsibility and ownership. You can't pay your kids $15,750 for organizing your office one time, your good buddies over at the IRS will catch onto that one pretty quickly. But you can pay them reasonable wages for legitimate work: general office tasks, social media management, even things as simple as modeling your brand to help with content creation, which is what we did with our son.

Important note: Details vary based on your entity type, your child's total income, and payroll requirements. Run your plan by a CPA before implementing. Also check current gift tax limits—as of 2025, a married couple can each gift their children $19,000 tax-free. All of that money that should be flowing into your children's banking-style policies to help create generational wealth.

Shift the Mindset: From Taxpayer to Tax Planner

"The tax code is a series of incentives for people who do what the government wants them to do." – Tom Wheelwright, *Tax-Free Wealth*

Let that sink in for a second.

The U.S. tax system isn't just a collection agency. It's a system of rewards. It gives you incentives when you do things that stimulate the economy, like:

- Starting a business.

- Providing housing.

- Investing in energy or agriculture.

- Hiring employees.

- Creating retirement plans.

- And yes, even owning certain types of life insurance.

So what if you could structure your financial life in a way that aligned with those incentives? What if, instead of trying to "hide" from the IRS, you worked *with* the rules they've already written?

This is what the wealthy have been doing for decades. And it's what we help clients begin to do as we start taking them through the four steps of the Legacy Lifestyle Process.

Case Study: Two Entrepreneurs

Let me show you what this looks like in practice. Say we have two entrepreneurs, Sarah and Mike. They both make $150,000 a year from their businesses.

Sarah's approach: She hires someone to prepare her taxes once a year. When March rolls around, she gets hit with a $30,000 tax bill and scrambles to figure out how to pay it.

Mike's approach: He builds a proactive strategy with a team that helps him:

- Set up an S corp structure.

- Use his whole life policy as a business asset.

- Deduct expenses like home office, mileage, meals, and travel.

- Employ his spouse and children.

- Take advantage of provisions like the Augusta Rule.

- Contribute to tax-advantaged accounts before year-end.

When tax season arrives, Mike owes just $8,000, and he's already planned for it.

Same income. Same rules. Completely different outcomes. The difference? One person was strategic about their planning; the other wasn't.

The Role of Family Banking in Tax Planning

One reason I'm such a strong advocate for building a family banking system is that it's not just a growth strategy—it's also a tax strategy.

Here's why:

1. Tax-Free Access

Properly structured whole life policies grow tax-deferred and, when used correctly, allow you to access cash tax-free through policy loans.

That means you can:

- Fund a business.

- Pay off debt.

- Invest in real estate.

- Build passive income streams.

All without triggering a taxable event on those borrowed dollars. (Note: Gains outside the policy on borrowed funds are still taxable.)

2. No Contribution Limits

Unlike 401(k)s or IRAs, there are no strict annual contribution limits. You're not capped at $7,000 or $23,500 per year (2025). If structured correctly, you can contribute significantly more capital while maintaining access without interrupting compound growth.

3. No Required Minimum Distributions (RMDs)

With IRAs, the government forces you to start withdrawing money (and paying taxes) once you hit seventy-three. With your family banking system, there are no forced withdrawals. You decide when and how to use your money.

4. Tax-Free Death Benefit

The death benefit passes to your family income-tax-free, so more of what you've built stays with your loved ones. Combined with a properly structured family trust, you can turn a one-time payout into a multi-generation wealth plan while avoiding probate.

Note: Work with qualified estate-planning and insurance professionals to set proper ownership/beneficiary designations and ensure funding stays within tax and MEC guidelines.

You Probably Need a Team

I'll say it again: I'm not a CPA, and I don't give tax advice.

But I *do* help my clients build a team that allows them to be proactive instead of reactive. Because the truth is, if your CPA is just filing your taxes and not helping you plan, you don't have a tax strategist. You have a historian.

Here's what an effective team does:

- Quarterly check-ins to adjust for income changes.

- Entity structuring to protect income and assets.

- Retirement plan implementation.

- Review of tax-efficient charitable strategies.

- Integration with family banking for liquidity and leverage.

And it's more affordable than you might think. I'm not talking about hiring a $500-per-hour CPA from Wall Street. I'm talking about assembling a smart, practical team that fits your income and goals. The idea is that this should be accessible to regular people. When I was starting out and basically broke, "accessible" also meant "affordable."

Thought Exercise: Your Tax Legacy

Take a moment to reflect on these questions:

- Have I ever truly planned my taxes, or just filed them?

- How much money have I unknowingly left on the table?

- If I could reduce my tax bill by 20 to 30 percent, where would I redirect that money?

- What would it feel like to look forward to tax season instead of dreading it?

Now imagine your children inheriting not just your wealth, but your tax strategy. What if you could pass down clarity and confidence instead of confusion and stress?

Implementation:
Three Steps to Get Started

1. Start Tracking

- Use affordable tracking tools like Quicken (cheap and works on both your phone and computer).

- Categorize every dollar—clarity is the first step to control.

- Quicken will help with categorization, or you can use our free budget template.

2. Form a Legal Entity

- Talk with a professional about whether an LLC, S corp, or C corp makes sense for your situation.

- We have a great team ready to help, and the initial conversation is always free.

- This unlocks new deductions and protection opportunities.

3. Schedule a Strategy Call

- Connect with people who understand proactive tax planning.

- Ask about coordination between infinite banking, legal structure, and business income.

- Get a comprehensive plan that works together.

Final Word on Taxes

Remember, the government isn't incentivized to teach you how to reduce your taxes. But they do reward you if you take the time to learn.

This chapter isn't about shortcuts or loopholes. It's about taking ownership of your financial future. Because you deserve to keep more of what you earn. You deserve to stop living in fear of April 15th. And you deserve to build a plan that works for you, not just the IRS.

Let this chapter be your wake-up call to stop overpaying and start reclaiming control.

LEGACY PROTECTION

A Legacy That Lasts

"The goal isn't to live forever, but to create something that will."

- CHUCK PALAHNIUK

When most people think about legacy, they think about money—wills, trusts, and assets passed down. But a true legacy goes much deeper than that. A real legacy is your story—the values you lived by, the beliefs you held dear, and the lessons you taught through action and intention. It's how your children remember you, and how your grandchildren are shaped by decisions you made long before they were born.

If you've made it to the end of this book, it's clear you're not just focused on wealth—you're focused on keeping it, protecting it, and passing it on. This is where real strategy comes in. Because the truth is, building wealth is only half the equation. Keeping it protected from life's biggest risks—aging, illness, taxes, and poor planning—is what ensures your legacy actually lasts.

The Overlooked Threat: Long-Term Care

Would you believe that most families underestimate how devastating long-term care expenses can be? According to the U.S. Department of Health and Human Services, nearly 70 percent of people over age sixty-five will require some form of long-term care in their lifetime.[17] That number jumps up to 92 percent if both you and your significant other are still alive. According to Genworth's Cost of Care Calculator (2024), the nationwide average daily cost for a shared nursing home room is $305 a day, totaling about $111,325 per year.[18] It's important to note that Medicaid typically covers shared rooms only, not private accommodations.

Here's the problem—without a plan, those expenses don't just drain your income; they cannibalize your savings, your retirement, and even the inheritance you worked your whole life to leave behind. I've seen it firsthand: One unexpected health event can erase decades of financial progress in a matter of months.

That's why, for my family and the clients I work with, long-term care coverage isn't optional—it's essential. And when it comes to designing that protection, there's one company's product that stands far above the rest.

Here's why: Unlike traditional LTC policies that work on a "use it or lose it" basis, OneAmerica's asset care is built on the same chassis as whole life insurance. That means your premium dollars don't disappear if you never need care—they continue compounding

---

17   U.S. Department of Health & Human Services, "How Much Care Will You Need? Long-Term Services and Supports for Older Americans" (Administration for Community Living, February 18, 2020), https://acl.gov/ltc/basic-needs/how-much-care-will-you-need
18   Genworth Financial. *Cost of Care Survey 2024*. Richmond, VA: Genworth Financial, 2024. Available at: https://www.genworth.com/aging-and-you/finances/cost-of-care.html

inside a guaranteed, permanent policy that will either provide living benefits for care, access to cash to spend freely, or a tax-free death benefit for your family.

Even better, asset care allows you to use the same dollars for three purposes at once:

- **Long-Term Care Coverage:** Access benefits for chronic or terminal illness.

- **Life Insurance Protection:** Leave a guaranteed, tax-free death benefit.

- **Cash Value Growth:** Keep your money working even while protected.

That's leverage—and it's why I tell every client: The best time to secure LTC protection is as soon as you're eligible—typically around age thirty-five. Waiting only makes it more expensive and limits your options. Think of it like locking in your financial peace of mind early, while your health and insurability are still on your side. Believe me, it's far more affordable than you think.

If there's one thing I hope you've taken away from this book, it's that the wealthy build their fortunes by leveraging a small amount of their own dollars to gain access to a large amount of someone else's. If there were a 70 percent to 92 percent chance that something was going to happen to me that could cost well into the six figures, I'd much rather use someone else's money to cover it than drain my own hard-earned wealth. That's exactly what long-term care planning does—it lets you protect your assets and your family's future using leverage instead of liquidation.

Protecting the Family Legacy Through Trusts

Once your protection plan is in place, the next step is ensuring everything you've built is organized and directed properly—that's where a family trust comes in.

A well-designed trust doesn't just distribute money—it defines purpose. It creates guardrails for how your wealth is used and ensures that your values continue guiding your family long after you're gone. A trust can protect your assets from probate, creditors, lawsuits, or even family disputes. But more importantly, it preserves your intention—so that wealth is not just inherited; it's stewarded.

Proverbs 13:22 says, "A good man leaves an inheritance to his children's children." That inheritance is more than financial. It's emotional, spiritual, and educational.

When Amanda and I sat down to create our family trust, we didn't just focus on who would get what. We focused on why. Why do we work so hard? Why do we live the way we do? Why it matters to pass this down, not just to our son, but to the generations after him.

In our trust, we included more than legal instructions. We added a family constitution—a mission, vision, and creed. We outlined:

- The values we want passed on.

- The causes we want supported.

- The mindset we want cultivated.

- How we want future children and grandchildren to think about money.

A trust built with intention becomes more than a document—it becomes a road map for your family's future.

Bonus: Download Your Family Trust Blueprint

As a gift to help you put this into practice, we've included a free downloadable trust-building document below. Inside, you'll find:

- A template to outline your family mission, vision, and values.

- Sample questions to ask yourself and your spouse or partner.

- Examples from our personal family trust.

- A guide on aligning your trust with your financial strategy.

Download it here: legacylifeprocess.com/legacy-builder-outline

You don't have to be a millionaire to build a meaningful family legacy. You just have to be intentional. The things we do today become the stories they tell tomorrow.

When you model discipline with money, when you take time off to be present with your family, when you prioritize giving back, learning constantly, or choosing character over convenience—those moments build the foundation your legacy stands on.

"Legacy is not leaving something for people. It's leaving something in people." - Peter Strople

CONCLUSION

I didn't write this book to convince you that my way is the only way. I wrote it because I wanted to help. I was tired of waking up every morning with no real plan, with no idea how I was going to provide for my wife and give her the life she deserved.

I'm just a regular guy. But then I realized—so is basically everyone else.

Did you know approximately 80 percent of U.S. millionaires are first-generation? That means they built their own wealth. If the majority of new millionaires are becoming wealthy through their own efforts, that means I have a chance and so do you. That light at the end of the tunnel was all I needed.

I was able to build the life I wanted because I was willing to do the things necessary to deserve that life. If you're willing to do those things, I believe you'll end up exactly where you want to be as well.

If you're ready to start building your ideal life, it's time to put in some intentional work. That includes reading, listening to podcasts, finding a coach or mentor, attending events, and giving up time spent on things that won't move you forward so you can focus on things that will.

Nowhere in this book did I say it would be easy. But I know it's possible, and it's absolutely worth it.

Your Next Step

The ball is in your court. The tools are in your toolbox. It's time to get to work.

If you want help, I'd be honored to coach, teach, and mentor you—but only if you're willing to put in the work. Time with my family is too valuable to waste on someone who isn't willing to fight for what they want.

If you can follow directions, get educated, and stay dedicated, I'd love to help you create a plan to take you *From Regular to Rich* because I know you deserve it.

Visit my website and book a free call. We'll discuss:

- What freedom looks like for you.

- Where you are right now.

- What systems and structures will best support your goals.

- What a real, tangible plan looks like to get you there.

- And where you can purchase *Becoming Your Own Banker* by R. Nelson Nash to dive even deeper into the concept of infinite banking.

I'll walk you through my Legacy Lifestyle Process, show you how family banking plays a role, and help you build a custom blueprint that makes sense for your life.

Book your free call here: LegacyLifeAndRetirement.com.

Thank you for trusting me with your time while reading this book. My hope is you were able to take at least one nugget away from these pages that you can apply in your life today to help you begin to move toward the goal of going *From Regular to Rich*.

As always, the information is free, but the knowledge is priceless.

To My Fellow Travelers

"If you don't design your own life plan, chances are you'll fall into someone else's plan. And guess what they have planned for you? Not much."

- JIM ROHN

Remember that money isn't the finish line. It's the tool you use to buy back your hours, to be present with your people, and to build a life that actually feels like *yours*. The systems you've been putting in place—budgeting with intention, building your Warehouse of Wealth, choosing cash flow over chaos—were never about a bigger account balance for its own sake. They were about control. Control of your calendar, your choices, and the way you move through your life.

I didn't realize that right away. For a long time, I chased "more" and assumed the feeling I wanted would show up eventually. It never did. The shift happened when I decided the real target wasn't flashy things that impressed others; it was *presence*. Not *someday*, but *now*.

That's when the freedom number from Chapter 2 stopped being a concept and started becoming a compass. Numbers don't create meaning, but they do make meaning possible. They tell you what it costs to live the way you say you want to live. Once you know the price, you can build the plan. For us, that life was focused around traveling all over the world and calling multiple different countries our home. If you're a traveler at heart like me, I believe this bonus chapter will bring you some real value.

What a Rich Life Actually Looks Like

Trust me when I say this: Money will not make you happy, *but* it will give you the ability to remove many of the obstacles in your life that make you unhappy. Before my son turned two, my wife and I had already taken him to ten countries. We've explored temples in Southeast Asia, beaches in Mexico, Christmas markets in Europe, and soaked up cultures far different than our own.

The question is, will he even remember a single moment of it? No, probably not, but we will, and those are the memories we will be able to cherish and share with him as he grows. More than the memories, those trips taught us something you can only learn by experiencing yourself: Wealth is relative, but richness is universal. You can live beautifully without spending recklessly when you design your life on purpose. We believe travel is one of the fastest ways to go *From Regular to Rich*, because it gives you something money can't buy: perspective.

This bonus chapter is all about turning the life you imagine into the life you actually live. Travel might not be everyone's dream, but for those who share my passion for exploring this beautiful planet we call home, consider this your invitation to start designing it intentionally.

In *Die With Zero*, Bill Perkins talks about maximizing life experiences, not just net worth. That quote really resonated with me because I've been trying to do exactly that for the past ten years.

Here are three simple steps to turn dreams into reality:

1. Define the life.

2. Price the life.

3. Build the wealth strategy to support the life.

Your freedom number exists to do exactly this; it turns dreams into numbers and gives your financial system a clear target to strive for.

Why This Belongs in a Wealth Book

I truly believe money without purpose is a trap. The system you're building, cash flow clarity, family banking, smart compounding—it's all a means to a richer life. For us, that means traveling together as a family. For you, it might be mountain adventures, coaching your kid's team, or building a business you love. The point is to find intentionality.

We've involved our son in this journey from early on. We talk about generosity, smart choices, and why we sometimes say "no" now, so we can say "yes" to what matters. That's how generational wealth actually begins; not just what you leave to your kids, but what you leave in them.

I've already mentioned this, but travel is a major life passion of mine. Because of that, I wanted to share some insight on what I've learned over the past ten years to hopefully inspire you to get out there and start seeing everything this world has to offer. I want to show you it's more affordable than you think. Sure, seeing the world when you "retire" will be great, but creating these life experiences either alone or with your family in your younger years will change so much of what lies ahead for you.

I'm about to go off on a tangent here. This probably wasn't what you were expecting when you picked up this book, but it was always a part of the plan. The goal wasn't just to write a book to teach you about improving your financial life. I wrote this book because I wanted to improve your entire life experience. My hope is that the information I provide ahead, gives you the ability to add at least one more amazing experience to your family's calendar each year. Because at the end of the day, the memories you create will be the only thing that truly matters when it's all said and done.

Travel is Part of the Plan (Not a Someday Reward)

Travel isn't some flex for us; it's part of our family culture. I've personally traveled to forty-plus countries in the last decade. Some of those trips involved dirt-cheap flights, crazy long layovers, shared hostels, and (as a six-foot-four human) spaces so small they felt borderline illegal. I've slept on dirt floors in northern Vietnam and in beds so comfortable in Prague I thought I'd died and gone to heaven. I believe those early "on the cheap" adventures helped shape the man I am today.

Your travel DNA changes as life changes. You grow, your family dynamics shift, your body starts to ache in places it didn't used to as a youngin, but oftentimes your budget is a bit larger than it once was as well. These days, we're still "value travelers," but we aim our dollars at places where they stretch much further: South America, Southeast Asia, and Eastern Europe, to be specific. That's how we squeeze in a little more comfort without spending like crazy.

Here's how we make travel realistic, and repeatable.

Decide What Kind of Traveler You Are (This Season)

Not forever. Just for this season of your life.

- **Budget Traveler:** You'll trade comfort for cost. Longer layovers, public transit, hostels, and street food, all for the goal of getting the opportunity to create the experience. I have so many incredible memories during this season of my travel life, don't shy away from it.

- **Value-Maximizer (Family Mode):** You want clean, safe, and comfortable, with a kitchen and laundry. Apartments instead of hotels, walkable neighborhoods that are stroller friendly, and off-peak travel times so you don't end up losing your kids in the massive crowds. This, for the most part, is our current travel situation, and, yes, we now use a leash backpack on our two-year-old (if you know, you know).

- **Convenience Traveler:** You want tasteful upgrades, priority lines, lounges, excursions, and boutique stays, all without lighting money on fire. We frequent this style of travel as well, especially when visiting our budget destinations. Don't be afraid to bounce between styles based on your upcoming destination.

The Four Levers That Make Any Trip Affordable

1. Where you go

2. When you go

3. How long you stay

4. How you fly and where you stay

Pull any two of these levers hard and your costs can drop dramatically. Pull three and you'll be shocked how far your dollars stretch. If seeing the world is on your bucket list, don't wait. It can be far more affordable than you think when planned strategically. Next up, I'll introduce you to a few tools we use to help to lower the cost of the two most expensive items: flights and hotels.

Our Flight Playbook (Real Tools We Use)

1) Going (formerly Scott's Cheap Flights)

Going is our secret weapon for airfare. I'm not exaggerating when I say this service has saved us tens of thousands on tickets. We get a "killer deal" alert, book it, and figure out the details later. It works best if you have a little, or a lot, of flexibility.

- **Free vs. Paid:** There is both a free and paid version of this subscription. I'd highly suggest getting the paid version (Premium) if you're looking for deals out of the country. It's cheap (around $50/year). You can try it for free, but I guarantee you it will end up being well worth the cost.

- **Set Multiple Home Airports:** The paid version will allow you to select multiple airports as nearby hubs so you can be sure to receive deals for more places than just your local airport. Plus, you'll have access to both domestic and international deals, which is by far the best bang for your buck. My suggestion, add any airport near you that you can either drive to or take a short and cheap flight to.

- **Move Fast:** Deals usually last twenty-four to seventy-two hours. If you have a bit of flexibility in your life, I'd suggest the "book now, plan later" strategy. Believe me, if you have the ability to book a flight to Paris, France, *not* Paris, Texas, for $400 round trip, you'll figure the rest out later.

- **Don't Worry, You've Got Time:** A lot of the deals end up allowing you to book six to ten months out, which was a huge bonus for us because not only did it give us time to plan, but it also gave us time to save up and stay motivated because we knew something amazing wasn't too far ahead. So, make sure you book in the twenty-four-to-seventy-two-hour window, but also feel free to not actually plan to go until six to ten months from now if that makes you a little more comfortable.

We've used Going at least twenty-five times in the past ten years, routinely saving $400 to $1,000 per ticket. Not only do we still use Going today, but we tell everyone we know about it because, damn, flights are expensive these days (thanks, COVID). One of the best ways to get rich and stay rich is to refuse to pay more if you don't have to. Below I've included a chart of the tier levels offered by Going and what they include at the time this was written.

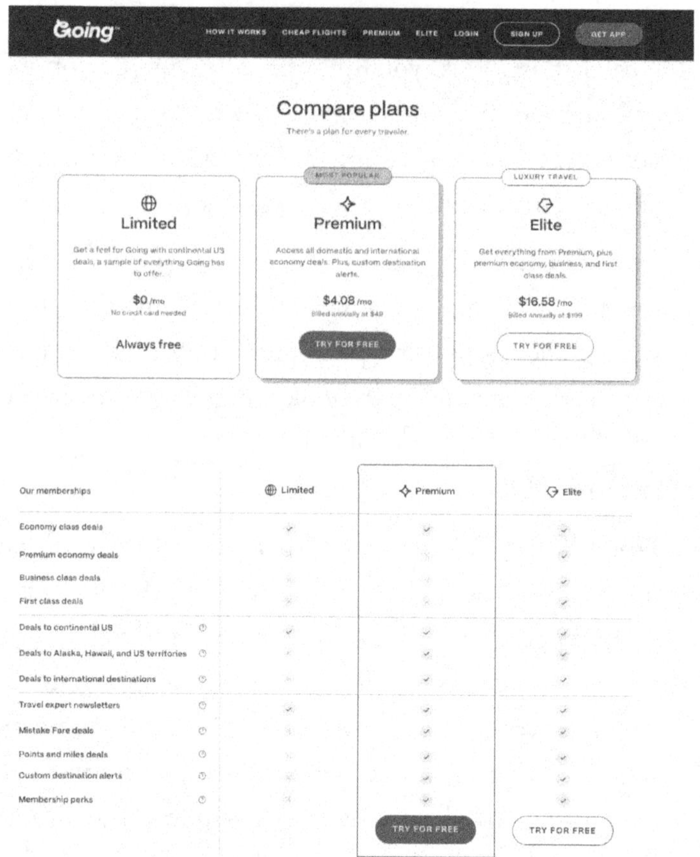

2) Google Flights "Explore/Anywhere"

If booking a surprise flight stresses you out but you still want to travel, the next best thing to do is to use the Google Flights Explore/Anywhere feature. Plug in your dates (or flexible dates), leave the destination open, and let the map show you cheap options all around the world. Obviously we don't always get a deal from Going for exactly where we want to go or when we want to go, but when that's been the case, we've turned to the Explore feature on Google Flights and it's worked like a charm.

Pro tip for international travel: Fly to the cheapest hub in the region (Europe/Asia), then book with one of the local budget carriers to reach your final destination. The savings can be drastic.

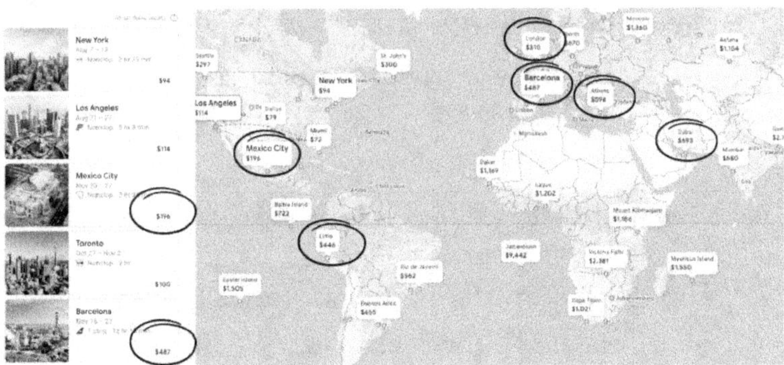

Points and Cards: Use Them Like a Pro (Not a Victim)

By now you know credit cards can be problematic if you don't have cash flow discipline. But when used correctly, they're powerful tools for reducing travel costs.

If you can't pay in full every month, don't play this game. Compounding works both ways—don't let it work against you.

Our Starter Setup (one to three cards maximum)

Capital One Venture X (Annual Fee $395)

- **Why:** Easy "cash-like" redemptions plus strong lounge access and solid transfer partners. The lounge access is clutch when traveling (free food and drinks).

- **How you earn:** Flat rewards on everything, plus boosted earnings on travel (10x miles on hotels and rental cars, 5x on flights, 2x on other purchases). This is our everyday spending card.

- **How you use:** Either "erase" travel purchases you've made, or transfer to partners when that provides better value.

Chase Sapphire Preferred (Annual Fee $95)

- **Why:** Great transfer partners, especially Hyatt (hotel value king) and airlines like United/Southwest. Strong travel protections and no foreign transaction fees.

- **How you earn:** 5x points on travel through Chase portal, 2x on other travel, 3x on dining/delivery/takeout

- **How you use:** Transfer to Hyatt for exceptional hotel value, or book through Chase portal. Solid, flexible foundation card.

Amex Gold (Annual Fee $325)

- **Why:** Point monster for dining and groceries (especially valuable for families).

- **How you earn:** 4x points at restaurants and U.S. supermarkets, 3x on flights booked directly with airlines, 2x on prepaid hotels.

- **How you use:** Transfer to airline partners (Air France/KLM, British Airways, Delta partners) for international flights; avoid low-value gift cards point exchanges.

Note: Offers change. Always check current bonuses and fees before applying.

The Sign-Up Bonus Strategy

- Pick one card that matches your spending patterns.

- Align the minimum spending requirement with expenses you already have: insurance premiums, medical bills, home repairs, planned travel.

- Don't force purchases. The bonus should come from redirecting existing spending, not adding new expenses.

Quick Example

You get a card with a 60,000-point welcome bonus after spending $4,000 in three months (using bills you already had). Those 60,000 points can cover two round-trip economy tickets to Mexico/Caribbean or several nights at a quality hotel. Stack this with a

Going.com deal and you're paying peanuts for a family trip you thought was out of reach.

Earning Responsibly

- Put every planned expense on the card that earns the most in that category.

- Keep utilization under 10 percent; pay before the statement closes if needed.

- Autopay in full. No exceptions. Late fees and unnecessary interest nuke all the "free" flights.

- Remember, before swiping, ask yourself: *Does this move me closer to my goal?*

Extra Protections You Actually Want

Many travel cards include:

- Trip delay/cancellation coverage (Venture X, Sapphire Preferred, Amex Gold)

- Primary rental car insurance (Venture X, Sapphire Preferred)

- Lost/delayed baggage coverage (Venture X, Sapphire Preferred, Amex Gold)

These perks can be worth hundreds when stuff goes sideways, so make sure to know what your card offers so you can be getting the most out of it.

Rules to Live By

1. If you don't have the cash, you can't afford it.

2. Use your card as a replacement for cash you already have, not future money you hope to have.

3. Autopay in full every month. No exceptions.

4. Know your *why* before you buy.

Hopefully these tips and tricks give you the ability to see more of this beautiful planet and create more incredible experiences with the people you love most.

My Invitation to You

Here's my invitation: Stop waiting for permission to live the life you already said you wanted. Your freedom number is the compass. Your Warehouse of Wealth is the engine. Your calendar is the canvas. It's time to get to work.

If you're financially able, I challenge you to do these three things within the next seventy-two hours:

1. Pick a date for your next meaningful experience (a weekend, a week, a day with your people).

2. Move money into your travel/experiences fund automatically, even if it's small—start building the habit now.

3. Book one non-refundable piece—momentum beats perfection.

Your kids won't remember your spreadsheets; they'll remember who you were with them. And you'll remember how it felt to buy back hours and spend them on what matters.

That's the whole point of this system: Presence, not pressure. Design, not drift.

If there's one thing I've learned, it's that the richest moments in life rarely cost money. They cost awareness. They cost courage. They cost intention. The view from a mountaintop, the laughter of your kids in a hotel pool halfway across the world, or the peace of watching the sunrise with the person you love most—those are the dividends of a life designed on purpose.

Money just gives you the ability to collect more of them.

I wrote this book because I wanted to help regular people—people like you and me—realize that freedom isn't reserved for the few. It's available to anyone who's willing to learn the rules, take control of their cash flow, and start moving with intention. If you take anything away from these pages, let it be this: **You have everything you need to create a life full of richness and meaning.** You don't need to be perfect. You just need to start. Start recovering what's yours. Start building your family bank. Start saying yes to experiences that feed your soul. Start teaching your kids not just how to earn money, but how to make that money matter.

Your journey *From Regular to Rich* doesn't end here—it begins.

And when you're sitting on that flight to your next adventure, or watching your family banking system grow, or just enjoying a quiet moment knowing your family's future is protected, I hope you remember this truth: **You designed this. You built this. You earned this.**

So take the trip. Write the story. Live the legacy.

Because true wealth has never been about the numbers—it's about waking up each day free to live life exactly how you choose.

Final Words

Most people don't choose to be stuck—they just never found a better plan. My hope is that this book has given you one. A plan for freedom, not just finances. A system that puts you back in control of your time, your choices, and your future. You don't need to have it all figured out; you just need to take the first step. Every system starts small, every legacy begins with one decision, and every rich life starts with the belief that you and your loved ones truly deserve more.

My hope is that this journey doesn't just lead you to more money, but to a life where you feel genuinely content. Where you're no longer chasing "happiness" as something always out in front of you. No longer searching for "meaning" as if it's hiding somewhere you haven't reached yet. No longer striving for "fulfillment" as a finish line you have to cross. Instead, you find yourself fully present in the life you're already living—grateful for simple moments, awake to the things that cost nothing, and at peace with the path that brought you here.

Chasing happiness will always keep it just out of reach. Choosing contentment allows you to finally exhale and experience your life as it is—right here, right now—and realize that, in many ways, you've already arrived. So go live it: fully, freely, and on purpose. Your journey from Regular to Rich has only just begun.

CLIENT TESTIMONIALS

"I couldn't be happier to have found Shawn when I did, except to say I wish I had met him sooner.

I reached out to Shawn to look into something I had been thinking about for two years and since that day he has been a weekly presence in my journey to the kind of financial independence I had been looking for. Full of knowledge, and relatable experience, it has been a very growth oriented period since I met him. From books to read, to podcasts and concepts to research, to meeting in person just to talk through what being your own bank is, and how to get there, Shawn treats you like you're his only client.

I am extremely grateful for his patience through this process, his constant motivation, and for being the catalyst for getting me on the true path to financial independence through Infinite Banking."

— Jake Reighard, Florida

Working with Shawn has been a very positive and eye-opening experience. From the very start, he has provided me with resources, education, and ongoing support that gave me a much clearer understanding of infinite banking and how it can truly benefit my family for years to come. Shawn has walked with me through every step of the process, making sure I felt confident, comfortable, and fully informed about the decisions I was making. He doesn't just present information; he takes the time to explain, answer questions, and make sure I understand how the strategies apply to my situation.

What stands out most is that Shawn is not only professional and knowledgeable, but he also comes across as a genuine family man who really cares about helping others. His passion for teaching and spreading the value of infinite banking shows in the way he communicates and the patience he has in guiding people through what could otherwise feel overwhelming. I've come away from this experience with peace of mind, knowing that I've put something in place that will create security and opportunity for me and my family. I would gladly recommend Shawn to anyone looking to take control of their financial future through infinite banking.

— *Devin Simmons, Florida*

Working with Shawn has been a standout experience. He took the time to explain the concept with patience, clarity, and kindness. He talked me through my hesitations in a genuine way. I feel like consulting with him was always a two way conversation. He's generous with his knowledge and acts as a true coach, meaning he's down to earth and genuinely in this for the right reasons. Because of that, our family (we purchased three policies) feels confident in our structure and ready to move forward with implementation. We trust that we're well set up for success. Highly recommended if you want someone who teaches, supports, and walks alongside you. I believe in him and value surrounding myself with like-minded powerhouse people like Shawn in my corner.

— Natalie Siedschlag, Tennessee

I highly recommend Shawn King, my financial coach for the past year, especially for anyone exploring the Infinite Banking Concept. He is full of recommendations and other sources to get the information across and through his contacts he will teach you how to become your own banker. Despite my unpredictable schedule and living on the other side of the world, Shawn always makes time for me and is consistently available when I need him. He's patient, knowledgeable, and genuinely cares about helping his clients succeed. Beyond his professionalism, Shawn loves to travel and is a hardworking family man dedicated to providing for his beautiful family—something that shows his integrity and dedication to his work. I couldn't ask for a better advisor.

— Travis Rose, Arizona

Book Suggestions

- *Becoming Your Own Banker 5th Edition* - R. Nelson Nash

- *Atomic Habits* - James Clear

- *Rich Dad Poor Dad* - Robert Kiyosaki

- *The Happiness Advantage* - Shawn Anchor

- DIBS On Your Money - Michael Kwong

- *7 Strategies for Wealth & Happiness* - Jim Rohn

- *The Case for IBC* - R. Nelson Nash and Robert Murphy

- *Profit First* - Mike Michalowicz

- *The Almanack of Naval Ravikant* - Eric Jorgenson

- *Who Not How* - Dan Sullivan

- *Rich Dad's Cashflow Quadrant* - Robert Kiyosaki

- *The Only Living Trust Book You'll Ever Need* - Garrett Monroe

- *The 7 Habits of Highly Effective People* - Stephen R. Covey

- *Think and Grow Rich* - Napoleon Hill

- *The Art of Exceptional Living* - Jim Rohn

- *The Psychology of Money* - Morgan Housel

- *Seven Generations Legacy* - Rachel Marshall

- *10x Is Easier Than 2x* - Dan Sullivan

- *You Need a Budget* - Jesse Mecham

- *Buy Back Your Time* - Dan Martell

- *The Purpose Driven Life* - Rick Warren
- *Permission to Spend* - Tom Wall
- *Value Creation Kid* - Scott Donnell
- *What Would The Rockefellers Do?* - Garrett Gunderson
- *Tax-Free Wealth* - Tom Wheelwright
- *The AND Asset* - Caleb Guilliams
- *The Richest Man in Babylon* - George S. Clason
- *From Passive to Passionate* - Brian Luebben
- *How To Buy Whole Life* - Ryan Griggs
- *Die With Zero* - Bill Perkins
- *Unlocking The Annuity Mystery* - Scott Stolz
- *The One Thing* - Gary Keller
- *The Gap and the Gain* - Dan Sullivan
- *Home Equity and Reverse Mortgages* - Harlan J. Accola
- *Titan: The Life of John D. Rockefeller, Sr.* - Ron Chernow
- *The World Walk* - Tom Turcich
- *OPM: Other People's Money* - Michael A. Lechter
- *Annuities for Dummies* - Kerry Pechter
- *The Evolution of Everything* - Matt Ridley
- *The Millionaire Next Door* - Thomas J. Stanley and William D. Danko
- *Vagabonding* - Rolf Potts
- *The 4-Hour Workweek* - Tim Ferriss
- *The 21 Irrefutable Laws of Leadership* - John C. Maxwell

Educational Podcast Suggestions

- ★ *The Cashflow Chronicles*
- ★ *The Banking Bros*
- ★ *Infinite Banking Initiative*
- ★ *Money School Podcast*
- ★ *Wealth Without Wallstreet*
- ★ *Life Success & Legacy*
- ★ *The Money Multiplier Podcast*
- ★ *Finding Financial Fitness*
- ★ *Farming without the Bank*
- ★ *Creating Tailwinds*
- ★ *Smart Money Parenting*
- ★ *The Money Advantage*
- ★ *Action Academy*
- ★ *Get Rich Education*
- ★ *Wealth on Main Street*
- ★ *The Infinite Wealth Podcast*
- ★ *Fun with Annuities*

Incredibly Grateful

Thank You For Reading My Book!

If you enjoyed the book, I'd be grateful if you'd take a moment to leave a rating and review on Amazon. Your feedback helps other readers find the book—and it helps me improve it.

I'm always looking for ways to increase the value I provide. If there's anything you loved, anything that wasn't clear, or any topic you want expanded, please include it in your review. I read every comment and will use your input as I work on the next edition.

Thank you so much!

www.ingramcontent.com/pod-product-compliance
Lightning Source LLC
Chambersburg PA
CBHW071507140726
47997CB00005B/1889